Peter Donigi

Indigenous or Aboriginal Rights to Property

A Papua New Guinea Perspective

International Books, 1994

338.995 DON

CIP-GEGEVENS KONINKLIJKE BIBLIOTHEEK, THE HAGUE

Donigi, Peter

Indigenous or aboriginal rights to property : a Papua New Guinea perspective / Peter Donigi. – Utrecht : International Books
With bibliography
ISBN 90-6224-988-4
NUGI 698
Key words: mining ; Papua New Guinea ; Juridical aspects / international law

© Peter Donigi, 1994

All rights reserved. No parts of this book may be reproduced, stored in or introduced into a retrieval system or transmitted in any form or by any means without the prior written permission of the copyright owner or the publisher.

International Books,
Alexander Numankade 17,
3572 KP Utrecht,
The Netherlands, tel: +31 30 731 840

For all those who are yet to be born,
May this be evidence that I tried.

For all those who are alive,
May this inspire renewed efforts.

"All those that do unrighteously, are an abomination unto the Lord thy God."
Deuteronomy 25:16

"He that oppresseth the poor reproacheth his Maker."
Proverbs 14:31

Contents

Foreword 7
About the Author 9
Introduction 11

Part A
Indigenous or aboriginal rights to property: a Papua New Guinea perspective

   I   Introduction 16
   II   Where do I come from? 17
   III   Acquisition of title at international law 19
   IV   Historical basis of property law in Papua New Guinea 21
   V   The United Nations Declaration and Covenants 28
   VI   Aboriginal title 32
   VII   Papua New Guinea's Constitution 33
   VIII   Conclusion

Part B
Equality and participation

   I   Introduction 48
   II   Monticello proposal 51
   III   Conclusion 54

Part C
Appendices

   1   Commodore Erskine's Proclamation over Papua of 1884 58
   2   Imperial Charter for the Neu Guinea Kompagnie of 17th May 1885 62
   3   Contract between the Reich and the Neu Guinea Kompagnie of 7th October 1898 65

4	On the maintenance of international peace and security	71
5	On measures to prevent terrorism	74
6	On the code of crimes against peace and security	79
7	An introduction to the International Covenants on Human Rights	86
8	On Developmentism and Constitutionalism	90
9	The Constitution and Human Rights	100
10	Briefing paper: Papua New Guinea Common Carrier Pipeline Company	106
11	A chance for real PNG involvement in the oil industry	111
12	Fragile investor confidence and a nation's interest, by *John Millett*	114
13	Economic nationalism and foreign capital, an opinion by *J. J. Tauvasa*	119
14	PNG Mining & Petroleum Projects	125

Notes		129
A	Indigenous or Aboriginal Rights to Property: A Papua New Guinea Perspective	129
B	Equality and Participation	133

Bibliography	137
Select bibliography of court cases	137
Books and other materials	141
Abbreviations	144

Foreword

Governments of donor countries have determined preconditions to aid ranging from free, fair and periodical multi-party elections to recognition of all forms of democratic rights and installation of a free market economy.

Yet a synopsis of the developing countries which have achieved tremendous economic and industrial progress will show their track record as being dependent on political stability during the relevant period of change rather than on a multi-party system of government. It is also dependent on the political will of those in government to implement policies for the benefit of its population at large, sometimes adopting positive discriminatory policies to favour its less advanced section of the population.

Free market economies in any developing country require the promotion of individual rights, as opposed to the collective rights of the clan or the social unit. This entails the breaking down of traditional norms which have been passed down through thousands of generations and which have bound the clan or the social unit in a web with its own socio-politico-economic base. These traditional norms are substituted by individuality, but not by the required mental conditioning as is known to the populations of developed countries, producing in those countries just societies.

There is a fine line to draw between those who are advocates of free market economies and those who, though agreeing to free market economy as an ultimate goal, wish to limit individual freedom for the benefit of a recognised minority group. In this respect a Papua New Guinean politician is required to tread carefully through this quagmire of differing, sometimes opposing and powerful interests. It is not an easy task.

In Papua New Guinea, the problem is exacerbated by the fact that the Government claims a greater interest in mineral and petroleum resources under land which belongs historically and by customary law to the individual clan groups; clans which have not at any stage agreed to cede their interests to the State. There are a trichotomy of interests between the individual, the Clan and the State.

Papua New Guinea is a symbol of democracy at work at the other extreme. It is by the very fact of its being a multi-party, multi-cultural and multi-lingual society. It is not an homogeneous society. As a Melanesian society, it attempts to reach consensus in all its deliberations. A fair decision requires a fair degree of free exchange of views, ideas and opinions. Freedom to hold and publish opinions is a guaranteed right under the Constitution.

Peter Donigi's opinion published in this book, though controversial, amounts to a positive analysis of the Government's lack of positive foundation or logic for its support for the current legislative scheme which vests ownership of minerals and petroleum resources in the State. The origins of these legislations lie in the Australian mining laws and practice which have now been held by the highest court in Australia to be invalid. This book has created a basis for further dialogue and possible resolution of the problems currently facing Papua New Guinea. The opinion is a constructive critique – one that I hope our policy advisers can analyse and assess for the benefit of all Papua New Guineans. It also provides a guide for reflection for our legislators before they commit themselves to legislative amendments.

I commend the author for having highlighted the pressing issues in this book for our reference and collective consideration.

Right Honorable Sir Michael T. Somare C.H., M.P.[*]

---

[*] Sir Michael Somare was the first Prime Minister of the independent State of Papua New Guinea, from 1975 – 1980. He is presently an independent Member of Parliament for the East Sepik Province.

About the author

The author is a prominent Papua New Guinean lawyer who has practiced law in that country for over 20 years. Peter Donigi's working career ranges from being a prosecutor to legal advisor to the Department of Foreign Affairs on international law matters, Head of Mission to European Communities, Head of Trade & Economic Relations and Acting Secretary for Foreign Affairs and Trade, senior partner of Warner Shand – lawyers of Papua New Guinea, Ambassador and special representative to the United Nations. He is currently the Ambassador to Germany with concurrent accreditation to the Holy See.

He has attended many international meetings commencing with the Asia Pacific Law Students Conference in Singapore in 1970. He graduated from the University of Papua New Guinea at the age of 21. His first speech at the level of the United Nations was at Caracas, Venezuela at the age of 22 when he addressed the United Nations Conference on the Law of the Sea on behalf of the then United Nations Trust Territory of Papua New Guinea. He was attached to the Australian delegation to that Conference.

He has also held many voluntary offices including that of founding President of the Papua New Guinea Australia Business Co-operation Committee – the predecessor of the Papua New Guinea Australia Business Council – and the President of the Papua New Guinea Law Society, a position which he held for many years. For his services to law and the community he was awarded the honour of the Commander of the British Empire in 1989.

In 1991 he was selected from amongst many other professional nominees by the Commonwealth Foundation to be one of the twelve Commonwealth fellows of that year. He was nominated by the Commonwealth Lawyers Association. He was co-opted on to the Council of the Commonwealth Lawyers Association in 1992 and was formally elected to that post in 1993.

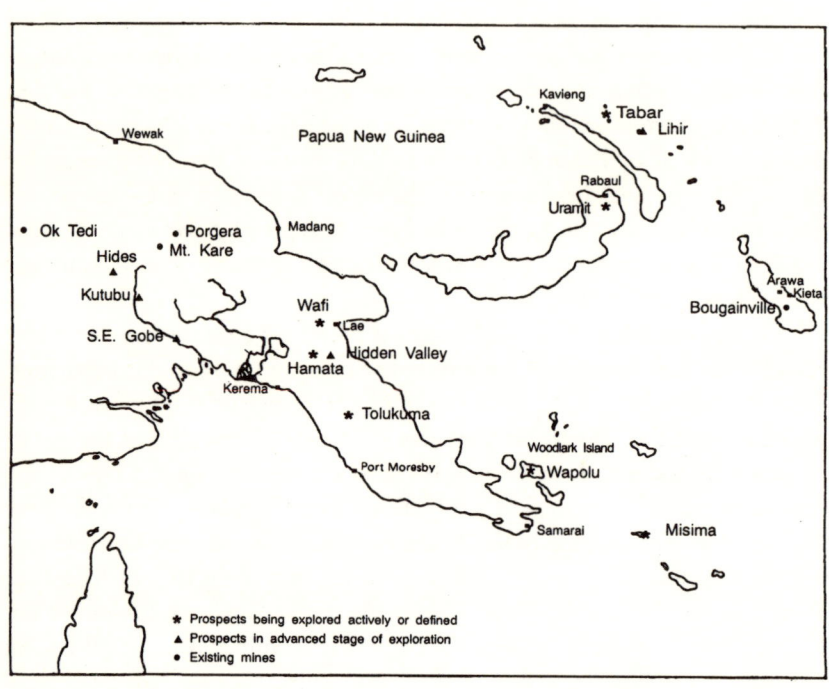

Introduction

Papua New Guinea, the land of the unexpected, where less than 60 years ago the population of its hinterland had never seen a European and where stone axes were still being used. The country of contrast thrown from the stone age era into the space age of technology, cars and flying machines; catapulted from the use of bows and arrows in the defence of tribal and clan land, water and territory to the use of guns and bullets and steel axes and knives.

This transformation was possible thanks to the huge wealth and natural resources that the country of many islands, languages and ethnic groups possesses. It has a land area that is larger than Germany with a population of 4 million, a vast internal sea (Bismarck Sea) and a large 200 mile economic zone. The natural resources include fish, natural forests, fauna and flora, oil, gas and minerals and land sufficient to support huge agricultural development. Papua New Guinea is endowed with the beauty of some of the world's rarest of flora and fauna, whose habitat is being increasingly encroached upon and destroyed by the quest for earning foreign exchange to provide goods and services for the expanding population. The country is becoming an increasingly popular target for conservationists and environmentalists.

New Guinea was administered by Australia under the United Nations Mandate after the first world war. Was it then a breach of the Mandate for the Australian government to authorise in the 1930s the exploitation of the gold from Wau and Bulolo in the Morobe Province of Papua New Guinea? Could there be a legal basis for a claim by the landowners against the Australian government?

Between 1949 and 1975, New Guinea was administered under the United Nations Trusteeship Agreement. During that period Australia extended its mining and petroleum laws to the trust territory such that small scale mining for alluvial gold was permitted only to holders of licenses issued by the Australian Administrator.

Australian laws did not recognise the rights of the traditional landowners to possession of gold or other mineral and petroleum resources. It was under that regime that the Bougainville copper mine was established.

On independence in 1975, the Australian legislative scheme was continued in Papua New Guinea. Since then, the Pogera gold mine, the Misima gold mine and the Ok Tedi gold and copper mine have been established. In addition the Iagifu oil fields have been developed and the country is now an oil exporter. Additional oil fields have been discovered since.

In the pipeline is the Mt. Kare gold mine, the Hidden Valley gold deposit, the Bulldog gold deposit and the Lahir Island gold deposit. The proven gas resources of the country are about 20 trillion cubic feet which can, if harvested, provide electricity to the country for more than a thousand years, based on current demand. Onshore exploration for oil and gas continue to be a big money spinner for the transportation industry and other service industries.

In this scenario of legislative authority given to the mining and petroleum companies to explore and develop the mining projects and petroleum fields, there is an increasing awareness amongst the landowners that something is extremely wrong, if the landowners cannot demand, as a legal and enforceable right, a fair share in the profits of the exploitation of the resources.

The Bougainville mine has been closed down since 1989. It was closed down by landowners who were dissatisfied with the arrangements concerning the distribution of a certain percentage of royalty payments. Their dissatisfaction has led to the hardliners taking up arms against the state and the mining company. Landowners of the Porgera gold mine have in the past also issued threats to close down that mine. The new government, elected in June 1992, issued statements in support of landowners and sought to increase its shareholding in the Pogera mine from 10 percent to 30 percent. An agreement was reached at 25 percent. The Mt. Kare mine was closed down for some time soon after it was due to be opened.

In any constitutional democracy, the rights of the people must be protected and upheld by the state. The current Papua New Guinean legislative scheme disenfranchised the landowners of their constitutional and internationally recognised right to property. It makes the landowners dependent on the goodwill of the state and on the mining and petroleum companies and denies them the right to a bargaining position. For as long as this regime exists, the new mines will remain hotbeds for future conflicts.

In this book, the rights of indigenous landowners of Papua New Guinea are reviewed within the current legislative and constitutional framework, in the light of existing international law on the subject of indigenous rights.

My father is the Chief of the Badeabus clan of the Arapesh linguistic group in the Sepik Province of Papua New Guinea. The clan has chosen me as the successor to my father, after his death. I am a lawyer by profession and I find myself confronted by a difficult conflict situation, as the official government position denies my people their basic rights. When I take on the leadership of my clan I may have to fight against the state to secure these rights, unless changes are made to the current legislative schemes. I hope that, by internationalising my concerns through this publication, I will influence the multinational companies now operating in my country and those in influential positions in its government to come to terms with the concerns of the indigenous peoples of Papua New Guinea.

Our concerns are those of all indigenous peoples throughout the world. My speeches at the United Nations in 1991 (reprinted in the Appendices) should not be seen as limited in their application to Papua New Guinea. Events around the world today could have been stayed if those in positions of influence were able to agree in advance on preventive measures. A cancer can only be cured by radical surgery. Should that be the prescription for international and intranational dissension?

In particular I have highlighted the fact that the international law principle of non-interference in the domestic affairs of a state has led states to sit on the sidelines and watch mass atrocities being waged by one warring side against the other. The events in, among others, Bosnia, Somalia, Ethiopia and Haiti are proof of that fact. The United Nations should mount fact-finding missions to trouble spots around the globe well in advance of the hostilities deteriorating into battlefields, with or without the consent of the states concerned. This sort of action should not be considered as interfering in the domestic affairs of a nation because it is in determining the cause of possible conflict that an impartial team could subsequently be established by the United Nations to assist in dispute resolution. It is prevention and not the cure which is crucial to world peace and harmony.

I subscribe to a very liberal interpretation of the term 'terrorism'. It is not limited to acts of violence. In its most liberal sense it applies to threats – by multinational companies or their respective industry organisations – issued to governments of developing countries to coerce them to adopt legislative policies to benefit the companies in their continued exploitation of the resources of those countries at the expense of the interests of the indigenous peoples. This includes the financing of the state's security forces to enforce these unfair and exploitative laws. Should multinationals and their industry associations be exempt from the international law principle of non-interference in domestic affairs of a nation? This and many other questions are raised in this book.

This book may also give insights to people in Eastern European countries who are struggling to understand the motives behind changes Western governments and multinational companies are likely to insist on as part and parcel of any restructuring process initiated in those states.

I hope that this book will provide inspiration to marginalised indigenous populations from Latin America to Australia in their continued search for change.

Part A
Indigenous or aboriginal rights to property: a Papua New Guinea perspective

Indigenous or aboriginal rights to property: a Papua New Guinea perspective

1 Introduction

I have over the last decade been quite vocal about the indigenous rights of the landowners in Papua New Guinea. In the process I have been branded with many a descriptive term by foreign capitalists masquerading as heaven-sent saviors of Papua New Guinea. When I was branded a *"carpetbagger"* I began to wonder whether the accusers knew the true meaning of that term. I console myself with the thought that I have traditional rights to hundreds of hectares of land and can settle on any portion of it without the obligation to pay rent or to purchase it. The same cannot be said of the foreign accuser intent on getting access to the riches.

When I was referred to as "a wild dog chasing wild pigs in the forest", I thought: "How odd, as it is my forest I will not get lost in it." The same cannot be said of the foreign accuser.

I hope the contents of this book will be educational to Papua New Guineans and indigenous peoples all over the world about their rights – the rights which some people in governments as well as international organisations seem eager to hide or, to use the common slang, shove under the carpet to facilitate the continued exploitation of the sub-soil resources of the indigenous landowners.

Hopefully this publication will convince certain people in positions of influence and authority that, in giving recognition to indigenous rights, the prospects for peace and good-neighbourliness can be promoted irrespective of the diversity of peoples within any single nation. To achieve this we, (the indigenous peoples, the state and the non-indigenous peoples) together need to apply "perestroika" – we need to restructure our political, social and economic institutions to serve our different and distinct peoples. It is evident that the institutions we now have are not suitable, and that if we persist with them, we shall lay the foundations for our people to turn against the repression instituted by governments and their advisors. We must settle all issues of ownership of land and the resources that it contains peacefully, before they get out of hand.

Our traditional cultures teach us to live with nature and to give due consideration to the interests of our future generations. I would like to think that my future descendants will not condemn me for trying. This publication will be testimony of my attempts to protect and to preserve, for them, their inheritance.

11 Where do I come from?

When anthropologist Margaret Mead wrote about the people of Wautogik village in the East Sepik Province of Papua New Guinea, she established that the name of their language was "Arapesh".[1] In her haste to receive recognition as being an authority on these people, she had in fact named the language of these people "the group of people". For "arapesh" in my language means exactly that.

Nevertheless "the group of people" still remains in some circles, including government circles, the name of my language. The point is that indigenous peoples throughout the world have never been given the opportunity to tell their own story or to write their own history or creation story. It has always been done for them by outsiders. The result is that they go to school to learn about what other people have perceived and written about them.

Foreigners who come to my country do so with a pre-conceived idea about my history which was written by a foreigner. They then promote that idea as the truth and are not prepared to listen to what I have to say. They change the burden of proof and place it on me to prove the contrary to what has been written by a foreigner. Why do I have to bear the burden of proof?

If a foreigner wants to defend the written works of a foreigner, he must bear the burden of disproving my history according to me. Many a time I hear foreign lawyers and mining company officials put forward this question: How do we establish the customary law of a given people in Papua New Guinea? I do not know the purpose of this question. I am truly flabbergasted and confounded by that question. Am I obliged to answer it just to please some foreigners' egotistical sense of righteousness? All I know is that I know the customary law of my people. The foreigners make it appear difficult in order to justify a foreigner making a complete study – possibly financed by an Aid Donor or the World Bank – to identify the customary law in respect to a particular issue at stake. It appears my word alone cannot be accepted, even by the Courts of our land. Only a foreigner can speak with authority about my customary law. Yet who determines and applies customary law in everyday situations?

I have a friend, a 1991 Commonwealth Fellow like myself, who is a Mohawk from Oka near Montreal, Quebec, Canada. His name is Daniel David, the Daniel David that Her Majesty Queen Elizabeth II at Buckingham Palace in my presence called the "naughty Mohawk" because he refused to swear allegiance to Canada in order to receive a Canadian passport for travel purposes. When I first met him at Cumberland Lodge, Windsor, England in May 1991, he looked at me wide-eyed and said "Are you *the* Peter Donigi, the person that I have heard so much about?" I did not know what to say. I was surprised that he would have heard about me in Canada. We immediately developed a bond of friendship. As the weeks went by and he was able to feel more at ease, he began to open his heart about the Mohawk stand-off with the Canadian army at Oka in 1990. I did not know, all that time in London and during our travels through the Solomon Islands, Vanuatu, Fiji, Western Samoa and Tonga in the South Pacific that he was very hurt and crying within to tell his story, the Mohawk story, the story of how his nation and his land was taken, raped, pillaged and sold by settlers in the guise of the Jesuit Missionaries.

It was months later in late November 1991, when I visited him and his family at Oka that he was able to feel free to tell me his story. He took me to "the pines", the site of the stand-off. It is people like the Mohawks and the Crees of Canada, other Indian nations of United States and the Aboriginals of Australia that inspire me to write this book. Although this book is dedicated to establishing the legal basis of the claim to the sub-soil resources beneath the land by the landowners of Papua New Guinea, the underlying question is still the same. Aboriginals of these nations have never ceded their rights to the natural resources of their land to foreigners. If we continue to allow non-aboriginals to tell our story, they will continue to hoodwink us into believing their story about us.

III Acquisition of title at international law

Historically, title to land or property can only be justified at international law if it was acquired by one of these four methods:
- Conquest,
- Occupation,
- Discovery, and
- Cession.

I will not review each method and determine its applicability to Papua New Guinea. Other writers have expounded on their inapplicability to the "new world".[2] Suffice it to say that conquest, occupation and discovery had no applicability to the new world and do not provide justification for denial of personal rights to property. In simple terms conquest involves the annihilation of one people by another and the forcible take-over of property by settlement. Occupation on the other hand can only be effected on ownerless property and the fact that the land was not settled because the owners practice and live a nomadic life, as in the case of the Australian aborigines, does not in itself justify extension of title by settlement or occupation. Discovery is not a valid concept as the original discoverers and occupiers were the aboriginal or indigenous inhabitants who were displaced by the Europeans.

These methods or concepts of acquisition of title to land or property do not apply to Papua New Guinea, where only three percent of the land area is owned by the state and the other 97 percent is owned by the indigenous landowners[3] in accordance with their own traditional or customary land tenure system. However, in the pursuit of defeating the rights of the original occupiers or indigenous inhabitants, the Europeans in pre-independent Papua New Guinea created a legal fiction to justify their claim to sub-surface riches to which they had no title. They created the fiction of *Crown right* and the principle of *eminent domain* and deemed all minerals and petroleum resources below any land to be the property of the Crown or the state. The state was, in turn, managed and controlled by a government which they had elected with the prime purpose of maintaining their claim, supported by a banner of democracy and good government. Legislation was passed which could effectively be interpreted and enforced in accordance with the debates they conducted in Parliament. In this way they were able to maintain their supremacy over the displaced indigenous peoples. Native lawyers are trained to argue and uphold the principle of *Crown right*, but are not taught the historical fiction on which this is based.[4]

The (non-indigenous) Vanuatu Chief Justice once commented, presumably in an attempt to influence change, that a constitutional rule that only traditional landowners could own land in Vanuatu had created "a ridiculous situation" in that country.[5] This sums up the attitude of many Europeans active in the Pacific and opposing the land claims of traditional owners.

The Europeans control the press, and any oppositional opinions which contribute to the general education of the population are inadequately publicised. The population which is immediately affected is promised employment, participation in health projects and education scholarships, winning the unsuspecting, uneducated population over to their side. But, as Con-Zinc Rio-Tinto of Australia discovered with its investments on the island of Bougainville[6] and Mt. Kare[7], both in Papua New Guinea, this is not an everlasting situation. And, when things go wrong, the press then publishes disparaging reports or survey reports conducted by those in control on the climate for investments,[8] and on law and order problems. Aid is tied to restructuring the bureaucratic machinery to establish elite squads – ostensibly to protect their investments but in reality to get indigenous peoples to kill each other – while they, like hungry scavengers perched on the tree tops, wait for the field to be clear enough to fly in and resume their stripping exercise.

In my country, the Europeans adopted in their entirety the same legislations which had been used in Australia to legitimise their claim over the rights belonging to the Australian aborigines. This resulted in the perpetuation of the fiction of Crown right, despite this right being historically founded on the English Crown's right to silver and gold – for coinage – and not to all minerals and petroleum as was done by those legislations. As gold and silver are no longer used in English currency, the fiction was all the more glaringly questionable.

The intention of the legislation was clear. The legislations were not applicable to land not under the control of or owned by the administering power, as will be seen later.[9] All land not bought by the administering power was therefore not under their control and could not be made subject to their legislation.[10] In practice, however, the administering authority proceeded to grant licenses to explore for minerals etc. over land[11] which was not under their control. No reference was ever made to the original Proclamation of Protectorates over the simple natives in which the then heads of state of England and Germany had promised, in writing, to protect the inhabitants of the islands of Papua and New Guinea. This included their rights to land and property.[12]

Accordingly, it should be stressed that, in reviewing the issue of indigenous rights to property in Papua New Guinea, it is not sufficient to apply *mutatis mutandis* the precedents, system of law or the legal rules to property rights of any country which had developed those rules of law as a result of its "assumed or perceived" acquisition of rights to land and property pursuant to one of those four methods. This excludes Australian rules of law and practice.[13]

IV Historical basis of property law in Papua New Guinea

Papua New Guinea is a nation which was created by the amalgamation or union of two territories. One territory was called Papua and the other was New Guinea. To understand my contention that the resources of Papua New Guinea, including minerals and petroleum under non-state land, belong to the indigenous landowners and not to the state, it is important to understand the historical basis of the law as regards property in the two separate territories.

Papua

The territory of Papua was proclaimed a Protectorate in 1884 by Commodore Erskine, for and on behalf of the British Crown, at a ceremony on the shores of Hanuabada village (now within the city of Port Moresby). The Proclamation he read out was in English. It is doubtful whether the Papuans who were gathered together for the ceremony understood the meaning of the Proclamation, but its words were nevertheless very clear indeed, leaving no room for doubt. The purpose of the Proclamation was provided in the preamble of the Proclamation as follows:

> "… for the protection of lives and properties of the native inhabitants of New Guinea and for the purpose of preventing the occupation of portions of that country by persons whose proceedings, unsanctioned by any lawful authority, might tend to injustice, strife and bloodshed,

and who, under the pretense of legitimate trade and intercourse, might endanger the liberties and possess themselves of the lands of such native inhabitants ..."[14]

In his explanatory speech following the reading of the Proclamation, Commodore Erskine emphasised further that

"... It is a Proclamation that from this time forth you are placed under the protection of Her Majesty's Government, that evil-disposed men will not be permitted to occupy your country, to seize your lands, or to take you away from your homes ... May the British Flag, which we have this day planted on these shores, be the symbol of their freedom – their liberty; and the Proclamation which I have read, the charter of their rights and privileges ..."[15]

This Proclamation cannot be read to amount to any form of acquisition of title to land or territory or an extension of sovereign rights or powers to Papua. It did not amount to any one of the internationally recognised forms of colonialisation and acquisition of title, namely, discovery, occupation or conquest. The Papuan Chiefs who were assembled to hear the Proclamation were never asked to cede their powers, authority or any portion of their land to Commodore Erskine or the British Crown. Accordingly, their territory could not be said to have been ceded to the British Crown.

The status of this Proclamation was the subject of various correspondence between the Colonial Office and the Law Officers. Letter No. 32 from the Law Officers to the Colonial Office, dated 11 December 1884, said:

"... That one of the reasons, if not the principal reason, which induced Her Majesty to assume a Protectorate in New Guinea had been the desire to *preserve the natives in the enjoyment of their lands, and to protect their persons and property* from outrage at the hands of unprincipled white men, and that with that object to obtain and enforce, for the present, full control of all settlement upon the protected area.
"... it therefore became important to consider whether the protected area should not be brought more directly under the sovereignty of the

Queen, *not with any desire for acquisition of the soil but as the best means of securing an effective and legal control over all persons resorting thereto.*"[16] (Italics are mine, for emphasis)

Letter No. 47, dated 20 July 1885, from the Law Officers to the Colonial Office quotes the question put to them thus:

"... that the native chiefs attended the ceremony of proclaiming the Protectorate, and that the principal men among them accepted from the Commodore a staff of Office bearing the Queens Head; but that although they were willing to recognise the Protectorate, they did not do any act equivalent to surrendering their country to Her Majesty. That in the absence of any settlement by British subjects, or any act of cession, it became a question whether territory which was added to the Queens dominions by Proclamation without the assent of the inhabitants might not be considered as being acquired by conquest."[17]

To which the Law Offices reported:

"... we do not think that under the circumstances stated in the letter the territory of New Guinea can be regarded properly as acquired by conquest or cession."[18]

Subsequent letters between the two offices related to issues of power to make laws, the method of making laws and whether the Governor of Queensland in Australia had overall authority over Papua. Even then the issue of applicability to "natives" of any proclaimed laws in the territory had never been properly dealt with. There was no question that these laws applied to British and foreign subjects within the territory. In practice, apart from allowing the Courts to settle disputes between natives, the proclaimed laws were not applicable to the native inhabitants whose activities were presumed to be regulated by their own traditional laws.

It was clear from those Colonial Office's letters of instruction that the people and their property would be protected against the unscrupulous and, in the terminology of Commodore Erskine, "evil disposed men" or, as in the Law Officers letter, "unprincipled white men". Erskine's pledge was reinforced by the Colonial Office's instructions to General Scratchley, the first Special Commissioner of the Protectorate, when he was ordered to explain to the Papuans that he was sent:

> "... To secure to them the safety of their persons, the enjoyment of their property, and particularly to protect them from being *deprived of their lands by force or fraud* ... If it shall be decided to allow Her Majesty's subjects or others to purchase land such transactions must in every case be conducted through ... [him] and that their wishes in these matters will be respected ..."[19]

This policy was implemented under successive administrative and subsequently legislative measures. Successive governors of Papua went to great pains to protect the natives and their lands and possessions. They did so by controls placed on acquisition of traditional or native land and property. Direct dealings in land were prohibited. Only the Governor could acquire land on behalf of the Crown. It is therefore clear that rights to land and sub-soil resources were never ceded to the British Crown and the Crown rights to all minerals, including the Crown metals of gold and silver, never became part of the law of Papua in its applicability to traditional or native land.[20]

New Guinea

The whole island of New Guinea was divided between the British, the Dutch and the Germans. Unlike the official ceremony surrounding the Proclamation of Papua as a British Protectorate, I am not aware of any record of an official ceremony conducted by the Germans in respect to the territory of New Guinea or Kaiser Wilhelmsland. It should be noted that the German government was not interested in the territory. The German government's decision to declare a protectorate was instigated by those of its citizens interested in the territory for the purposes of trade. Accordingly, what transpired was a Deed of Grant of Letters of Administration issued by the then Emperor of Germany, authorising the managers of the German Neu Guinea Kompagnie, which had plantation interests in the New Guinea Islands region, to exercise authority over its citizens and

> "... to create and maintain in the Protectorate such administrative institutions as will serve the promotion of trade and economic utilisation of the land as well as the establishment and strengthening

of peaceful relations with the natives and their civilisation, at the same time requesting that in order to achieve these aims it be granted by means of an Imperial Charter the right to exercise local sovereignty under our sovereignty, and in addition, the exclusive right to occupy and to dispose of ownerless land and to conclude contracts regarding land and land rights with the natives, under the supervision of our government ..."[21]

In 1898, the government of Germany entered into a contract with the German Neu Guinea Kompagnie to assume government control of the Protectorate of New Guinea. Clause 2 states:

"The Neu Guinea Kompagnie renounces in favour of the Reich the special property rights for the whole area of the Protectorate ... which were granted by the Charter and which it possesses by virtue of the same, to wit:
a the exclusive right to occupy and dispose of ownerless land ...;
b the right to ... mining for ores, precious stones, and combustible minerals ... not in the possession of natives or otherwise privately owned ..."[22]

This contract confirms that the Neu Guinea Kompagnie never had the power to explore and to win minerals from land owned by the indigenous peoples.

Land was, as in Papua, bought from the traditional owners for the settlers for their plantations by the Administering Authority. Indigenous or native title to land was therefore recognised and never disturbed by the Administering Authority. The right to minerals and petroleum was limited to that land already acquired from the indigenous populations.

Under the League of Nations Mandate, New Guinea became the responsibility of the Australian government after the first world war. After the second world war, it was administered under the United Nations Trusteeship Agreement with Australia. The terms of the Mandate and the Trusteeship Agreement are essential to the role, the responsibilities and the powers of the administering authority.

The International Court of Justice reviewed the issue of the Mandate for South West Africa (now known as Namibia) which was in the same category as New Guinea after the first world war. In a separate opinion, Sir

Arnold McNair was of the view that Article 22 of the Covenant of the League of Nations created a trust between the mandatory and the administered:

> "... The trust has frequently been used to protect the weak and the dependent, in cases where there is 'great might on the one side and unmight on the other', and the English courts have for many centuries pursued a vigorous policy in the administration and enforcement of trusts."[23]

He continued:

> "There are three general principles which are common to all these institutions:
>
> a that the control of trustee, tuteur or curateur over the property is limited in one way or another; he is not in the position of the normal complete owner, who can do what he likes with his own, because he is precluded from administering the property for his own personal benefit;
>
> b that the trustee, tuteur or curateur is under some kind of legal obligation, based on confidence or conscience, to carry out the trust or mission confided to him for the benefit of some other person or for some public purpose;
>
> c that any attempt by one of these persons to absorb the property entrusted to him into his own patrimony would be illegal and would be prevented by law."[24]

On sovereignty, Sir Arnold McNair said:

> "... The Mandates System (and the corresponding principles of the International Trusteeship System) is a new institution – a new relationship between territory and its inhabitants on the one hand and the government which represents them internationally on the other – the new specie of international government, which does not fit into the old conception of sovereignty and which is alien to it.
> "The doctrine of sovereignty has no application to this new system. Sovereignty over a Mandated Territory is in abeyance; if and when the inhabitants of the Territory obtain recognition as an Independent

State ... sovereignty will revive and vest in the new State. What matters in considering this new institution is not where sovereignty lies, but what are the rights and duties of the Mandatory in regard to the area of territory being administered by it. The answer to that question depends on the international agreements creating the system and the rules of law which they attract. Its essence is that the mandatory acquires only a limited title to the territory entrusted to it, and that the measure of its powers is what is necessary for the purpose of carrying out the Mandate.

"The Mandatory's rights like the trustee's, have their foundation in his obligations; they are 'tools given to him in order to achieve the work assigned to him'; he has 'all the tools necessary for such end, but only those'. (See Brierly in *British Year Book of International Law*, 1929, pages 217-219.)"[25]

Sir Arnold McNair also quoted the judgements of Chief Justice Latham and Justice Evatt of the High Court of Australia in the case of *Frost v. Stevenson* (1937) in respect to New Guinea. In that case Chief Justice Latham said:

"... Thus the title under which the territory is to be held as a mandated territory is different from that under which a territory transferred by simple cession would have been held. [Article 257 of the Treaty of Peace] shows that the intention was to achieve a transfer of a territory without making that territory in the ordinary sense a possession of a mandatory. A territory which is a 'possession' can be ceded by a power to another power so that the latter power will have complete authority in relation to that territory. Such a cession by a mandatory power would be quite inconsistent with the whole conception of a mandate. A mandated territory is not a possession of a power in the ordinary sense."[26]

Mr Justice Evatt said:

"It is quite fallacious to infer from the fact that, in pursuance of its international duties under the mandate, the Commonwealth of Australia exercises full and complete jurisdiction over the territory as though it possessed unlimited sovereignty therein, either that the territory *a* is a British possession, or *b* is within the King's dominions, or *c* has ever been assimilated or incorporated within the Commonwealth or its territories ...

"Therefore it can be stated that ... every recognised authority in international law accepts the view that the Mandated Territory of New Guinea is not part of the King's dominions. Over and over again this fact has been recognised by the leading jurists of Europe including many who have closely analyzed such matters in relation to the organisation and the administration of the League of Nations."[27]

Clearly, Australia had no complete sovereignty over the territory of New Guinea and its inhabitants. It therefore had no legal basis for passing legislations prior to Papua New Guinean independence which could deprive the indigenous peoples of their land or their rights to property. This would include the vesting of ownership of minerals or petroleum under individual clan land in the Administering Authority.

Thus it would appear that exploitation of minerals on unalienated land by foreigners, pursuant to the granting of mining permits or mineral leases issued by the Administering Authority, was, prior to Papua New Guinean independence, illegal.

It is therefore plausible for the landowners of the Wau and Bulolo area in the Morobe Province to mount a claim for damages against the Australian government for breach of trust. The Australian administration allowed a gold rush to take place in this region after the first world war.

Some lawyers[28] have argued that the government of the Independent State of Papua New Guinea inherited, on Independence Day, the rights to gold, minerals and petroleum from its predecessor in office, the Administering Authority. In this book I will attempt to clarify the point that the Administering Authority did not have the power in the first instance to alienate ownership from the indigenous peoples. In my opinion, the reasoning contained in this book defeats the contentions proffered by lawyers who support the vesting of ownership of sub-surface resources in the state.

v The United Nations Declaration and Covenants

The main documents which deal with "peoples" rights to property are the United Nations Charter, the Universal Declaration of Human Rights, the

International Covenant on Economic, Social and Cultural Rights, and the International Covenant on Civil and Political Rights.
The Universal Declaration of Human Rights says that:

"... no one shall be arbitrarily deprived of his property".[29]

The two International Covenants use identical language as follows:

"1 All peoples have the right of self-determination. By virtue of that right they freely determine their political status and freely pursue their economic, social and cultural development.
"2 All peoples may, for their own ends freely dispose of their natural wealth and resources without prejudice to any obligations arising out of international economic co-operation, based upon the principle of mutual benefit, and international law. In no case may a people be deprived of its own means of subsistence."[30]

These documents support the contention that the mining and petroleum legislations in Papua New Guinea, which arbitrarily declared ownership of gold, minerals and petroleum in, on or under land other than state land to be vested in the state, as amounting to deprivation of property rights of the indigenous peoples. They amount to deprivation of the indigenous peoples' (landowners/clans) "own means of subsistence", to use the language of the International Covenants.

The Declaration on Principles of International Law concerning Friendly Relations and Co-operation among States in accordance with the Charter of the United Nations is also of relevance. It sets out the duty of every state to "refrain from any forcible action which deprives peoples referred to in the elaboration of the principle of equal rights and self-determination of their right to self-determination and freedom and independence".[31]

The principle of equal rights and self-determination of peoples states:

"By virtue of the principle of equal rights and self-determination of peoples enshrined in the Charter of the United Nations, all peoples have the right freely to determine without external interference, their political status and to pursue their economic, social and cultural development, and every State has the duty to respect this right in accordance with the provisions of the Charter."[32]

All major United Nations documents use the term "peoples" and seek to distinguish between the rights of states and the rights of peoples. It is clear that "peoples" and "states" are not interchangeable words. Recognition is therefore given to the fact that several "peoples" can be found within a state.

What is the definition of "peoples"? It is clear from various works that a people must have a common tie or bonding factor. They must be easily identifiable. They must be distinct from other people. Thus a people can be identified by a common language, culture, race, geographical location or a combination of these factors. The Declaration of Principles for the Defense of the Indigenous Peoples of the Western Hemisphere states:

> "Indigenous groups not meeting the requirements of nationhood are hereby declared to be subjects of international law and are entitled to the protection of this declaration, provided they are identifiable groups having bonds of language, heritage, tradition, or other common identity."[33]

If language is to be the criterion, then Papua New Guinea is a nation of seven hundred or so peoples within the meaning of the various United Nations documents. Each language group in Papua New Guinea therefore has a right to self-determination pertaining to their political status and the pursuance of their economic, social and cultural development. The government of Papua New Guinea is bound by its membership of the United Nations to respect that right. To suppress that right would be a violation of its international duty.

If geographic location is to be the criterion then it is possible for each of the nineteen Provinces or the four regions to claim that right to self-determination. The right of the people of Bougainville to secede is therefore a right at international law and the government of Papua New Guinea cannot suppress that right. It is a right which must be exercised in a democratic manner, peacefully and without duress and force. What the government can do, however, is to convince the people of the virtues of the old adage "divided we fall, united we stand" and hope that in the exercise of their right to freely determine their political status, they will continue to be part of Papua New Guinea.

Dr. Otto von Habsburg (Prince), Member of the European Parliament, mentioned in his speech to a group of Ambassadors in Bonn, Germany[34] that when General Tito of Yugoslavia went to Austria he told the then Prime Minister of Austria that he (Tito) was the only Yugoslavian in the whole of Yugoslavia as all the others were either Bosnians, Serbs or Croatians. A country which is created without the necessary "will" of the people can never survive. Yugoslavia was an enigma. Its survival was a dire contradiction of the United Nations Declarations on Human Rights, of the right to self-determination and the right to development. It can validly be argued that the current fighting in what formerly was Yugoslavia is not a civil war but an international war involving the invasion of one country by the other. The United Nations has taken sides by imposing a ban on supply of arms to the nations that were invaded. By doing so, the United Nations has acted contradictory to the rights of the peoples to defend themselves (all armament factories are located in Serbia).[35]

I was attached to the Papua New Guinea Mission to the United Nations between August and December 1991. During this time I delivered several statements at the Sixth (Legal) Committee of the United Nations General Assembly. I reproduce excerpts of these statements, which expand on my argument for and on behalf of indigenous peoples, in Appendices 4, 5 and 6. In these statements, I promote the idea that the rights of indigenous peoples can be exercised within the territory of a state without consequent disruption and without carving the state into many independent states. To be able to achieve that, the government of the state party to the United Nations Charter must recognise the inalienable rights of the indigenous populations to their land and all the resources it entailed, their culture and their language. Above all, the state must establish a constitutional framework for giving effect to the obligations it has at international law to the various indigenous peoples within its territory. It must not suppress the rights of the minorities. Nor should it super-impose the ideologies of the majority or a powerful minority on other peoples within its territory. It is in diversity that the state can obtain its strength.

While preparing one of the speeches a compatriot reminded me of the fact that Lady Somare, wife of Sir Michael Somare, the first Prime Minister of Papua New Guinea, is a member of a distinct and probably the smallest language group in the East Sepik Province of Papua New Guinea.

It is claimed that the group has less than 2000 members. International law requires that the state preserves their identity, language and culture. Unfortunately, the current trend in the process of political, economic and cultural development in Papua New Guinea will result in assimilation of this and other small populations. Assimilation is equivalent to cultural genocide. Assimilation can also, in the course of several generations, legitimise illegal occupation of land or illegal acquisition of property or property rights.

VI Aboriginal title

In Papua New Guinea the claim to sub-soil resources by landowners is based, since time immemorial, on possession of the land surface. Accordingly, the non-alienated or non-government land is known as customary land. Its occupation and usage is determined according to the traditional custom of the landowning group, which, in all cases, is the clan. The mining industry and the foreign advisors to the government have argued that possession since time immemorial does not entitle the landowners to ownership of the sub-soil resources. They contend that traditional societies use land only for farming, hunting, gathering, burial and fishing and that they possess no concept of mining. Accordingly, as the traditional societies had no use of the sub-soil resources, they are not in a position to claim these resources as their own.

I am led to believe that recent anthropological research will disprove the theory that traditional societies made no use of sub-surface resources. Research has found an indication that some traditional societies in Papua New Guinea did conduct mining activities. Whether anthropological research proves previous mining or not, there is a more fundamental reason for me to discard the argument used by the mining industry. It is simply this. "Usage" of land alone has never been part of any known legal system throughout the world of conferring title to land. All major legal systems recognise "possession" as the ultimate in conferring title. The customary laws of all clans in Papua New Guinea also recognise "possession" as the basis of title. Accordingly, "usage" alone is a new criteria created and promoted by the mining industry to perpetuate their continued exploitation of the resources of the true owners. Are these the "evil disposed men" or the "unprincipled white men"[36] that Her Majesty undertook to protect the

Papuans against in 1884? The words of the 1884 Proclamation will come back to haunt the promoters of Crown rights and sovereign rights to subsoil resources.

"Possession since time immemorial" is therefore the true basis of aboriginal title to land and all that it entails, either at international law or at customary law. There have been a number of important judgements supporting this basis. For example, Chief Justice Marshall in the United States cases of *Johnson v. McIntosh*[37] and *Worcester v. Georgia*[38] recognised the legitimacy of aboriginal rights founded on possession.

VII Papua New Guinea's Constitution

Constitution is supreme

The Constitution is the supreme law of Papua New Guinea and all other subsidiary legislations are subject to its provisions. Where there is a conflict between the Constitution and the legislation, the legislation is not invalid per se but is unenforceable to the extent of its invalidity or its inconsistency with the provision of the Constitution. Thus, the mining and petroleum legislations, being subsidiary, are subject to the Constitution.

Several foreigners in the mining sector of Papua New Guinea and in the Government Department of Minerals and Energy promote the idea amongst our politicians, bureaucrats, landowners and others that what I am trying to do, in the court cases I have appeared in, is to get the Courts to amend the Constitution. A government officer, surprised to see me at a luncheon hosted by Mobil in honour of the mining sector in New York in November 1991, underlined this when he said to me:

> "Oh!! What are you doing here? Have you changed the Constitution of the United States yet?"[39]

This claim is a figment of their imagination and amounts to deliberate misinformation calculated to create opposition against me and the judicial processes in Papua New Guinea. The country and the government does not need people like that who deliberately distort the situation to cause dissension amongst its leaders and population.

It is a legitimate function of the Courts to interpret the Constitution and to apply it to any situation. It is not a function of the Courts to amend the Constitution. The mining legislation, if inconsistent with the Constitution, will be ineffective to the extent of its inconsistency.

My contention has been that the provision of the mining and petroleum legislations which vests ownership of gold, minerals and petroleum under customary land or land other than state land, in the state, is unconstitutional. It has always been my contention that the Constitution[40] is consistent with international law in that it prohibits unjust deprivation of property unless certain prerequisites are met. The mining and petroleum legislations are not only unconstitutional but are also contrary to international law as regards the rights of the "peoples".

Sovereign Right

Another argument which has been put forward by some Papua New Guinea lawyers is the sovereign right of the state, or the right of eminent domain as it is known in United States constitutional law. This argument, however, is based on a misinterpretation of United States law. Chief Justice Marshall, as I have already noted, was quite clear in developing the principles of native title in the United States. The principles he enunciated were:

> "1 Native title was a legal right based on the fundamental principle of prior possession. The Indians were admitted to be the rightful occupants of the soil, with a legal as well as just claim to retain possession of it.
> "2 Native title did not depend on any particular land-use or kind of settlement. Agriculture was never regarded as a prerequisite for native title, which was considered with reference to their habits and modes of life; their hunting grounds were as much their actual possession as the cleared fields of the whites; and their rights to its exclusive enjoyment in their own way or for their own purposes.
> "3 Native title did not exist in opposition to the complete, ultimate title of the United States (or the Crown). The government had the exclusive right to extinguish native title. But that title had to be considered as a form of property. Indian consent should be sought and compensation paid when the government exercised its right of pre-emption."[41]

The Papua New Guinea Constitution states the following on the sovereign right of the state:

> "The sovereignty of Papua New Guinea over its territory, and over the natural resources of its territory, is and shall remain absolute, subject only to such obligations at international law as are freely accepted by Papua New Guinea in accordance with this Constitution."[42]

This provision does not say that the natural resources within the territory of Papua New Guinea shall be the property of the Independent State of Papua New Guinea. Nor could it have said that as those "schooled" in international law and constitutional law would say otherwise. It is merely declaratory of international law which is recognised in the Charter of the United Nations. It is declaratory of the fact that in its relations with other countries Papua New Guinea as a nation has liberty of action within its territorial boundaries and over the natural resources within that boundary. That is to say that no other nation can claim the right to legislate over property or to exercise sovereign jurisdiction over the natural resources in Papua New Guinea.

An important pronouncement on sovereign right was made in the Nigerian case of *Amodu Tijani v. Secretary for Southern Nigeria*[43]. In this case, the British Privy Council stated that "a mere change of sovereignty is not to be presumed as meant to disturb rights of private owners ..." Thus, annexation or cession gave the Crown "political sovereignty" and not "proprietary ownership" in land and property.

Papua New Guinea was neither annexed nor ceded to the British Crown or the German Reich. There can never be any need to discuss the question of whether or not the indigenous landowners had ever ceded their right to land and property to the British Crown or the German Reich. The British Crown and the Australian Administration after the war therefore can never be deemed to have been in proprietary ownership of any other land than state land which had been purchased from the indigenous people and with their consent. They had no proprietary ownership of any other land, gold and other minerals. On independence the "political sovereignty" was transferred from the Australian Administration and became vested in the Independent State of Papua New Guinea.[44] The indigenous peoples' rights to land was never disturbed. In fact their rights were further entrenched and protected by the Constitution.[45] This is consistent with the following statement in the Constitutional Planning Committee Report which recognised indigenous ownership and distinguished the state's right to compulsory acquisition as applying only to foreign-owned properties:

> "Our own people are more fortunate than those in many other new States in that most still have their own land, their rights to which they rightly intend to protect most vigorously ... After very careful consideration we have decided to recommend that the constitutional protection of property interests should be limited to our own citizens. The interests of foreign citizens can be protected in a number of ways by the government of the day ... by legislation ... by agreement between government and the particular enterprise or by a general law concerning a certain type of property. Our aim is to give the government of the day sufficient flexibility to deal with acquisition of foreign owned property and payment for it in an appropriate way, according to the circumstances with which it is faced."[46]

It is in the exercise of that sovereign right and claim that Papua New Guinea arrested the United States' licenced fishing vessel "Danica" in 1981 for fishing illegally within Papua New Guinea's 200 mile economic zone. United States laws and practice at that time did not recognise our claim to the 200 mile economic zone.

The claim of sovereignty has been questioned by many indigenous peoples. Leroy Little Bear questioned the western legal opinion in a more succinct manner when he said:

> "When the courts and the government say that the Indian's title is dependent on the goodwill of the sovereign, and that the Indians' interest is a mere burden on the underlying title of the Crown, the question to ask is, 'Where did the Crown get its title from? And How?'"[47]

I might as well ask, where did the Crown or the Australian government get its power to terminate the rights of the landowners in Papua New Guinea in respect to sub-surface resources when all the documents which give them authority to administer the territory of New Guinea and the territory of Papua say otherwise?

The best explanation of the word "sovereign" is provided by Lord Aitkin in *The Avantzazu Mendi* case where he said:

> "By 'exercising defacto administrative control' or 'exercising effective administrative control', I understand exercising all the functions of a sovereign government, in maintaining law and order, instituting and maintaining Courts of Justice, adopting or imposing laws regulating the relations of inhabitants of the territory to one another and to the government ... In those circumstances it seems to me that the recognition of a government as possessing all those attributes in a territory while not subordinate to any other government in that territory is to recognise it as sovereign, and for the purpose of international law as a foreign sovereign State."[48]

Thus in simple English, a proper interpretation of the Papua New Guinea Constitution[49] should be that:

> "Papua New Guinea as an independent nation has power to do all those things stated by Lord Aitkin within its territory and has power to legislate and regulate the relationships between individuals and between individuals and the government in relation to the territory and the natural resources within that territory."

The Papua New Guinea Constitution therefore does not give the government of Papua New Guinea property rights over all natural resources in the country. It gives the state the political sovereignty or the power to legislate. The legislation, being a subsidiary document, remains subject to the substantive provisions of the Constitution.

Property Rights

The Constitution provided for the right to property. The relevant section states that:

> "... possession may not be compulsorily taken of any property and no interest in or right over property may be compulsorily acquired except by an Act of Parliament ..."[50]

The Constitution has also set out several preconditions, which must be complied with by passing an Act of Parliament. The property acquired must be required for a public purpose. The purposes and reasons have to be stated in the legislation. It is therefore implicit that the property to be acquired and the owners of that property must be identified and that compensation for the deprivation must be stated. The mining and petroleum legislations do not meet these criteria or preconditions and are flawed in many requirements. These are matters which have yet to be argued before the Courts of Papua New Guinea.

In looking at these issues one must also attempt to define the term "property". In the past, some promoters of indigenous rights argued that ownership of the surface of the land should be distinguished from ownership of sub-soil resources. This was the case in the draft Universal Declaration on Indigenous Rights, promoted by Erica Daes, Chairperson of the UN Commission on Human Rights Sub-Commission on Prevention of Discrimination and Protection of Minorities. My comments on that draft Declaration are contained in my Statement to the Sixth Committee of the UN General Assembly in respect to the draft articles on the code of crimes against the peace and security of mankind.

In that statement, after highlighting the contradictory paragraphs of the draft Declaration, I said:

> "There is no doubt that the indigenous peoples right to property is a fundamental right at international law. By distinguishing surface rights from sub-soil rights, we have not only discriminated against these 'peoples' but more importantly, taken away their right to future wealth, resources and their 'own means of subsistence'. We have by this draft declaration of indigenous rights qualified or restricted the meaning of the terms 'peoples' and 'property' as used in the Charter and the Covenants ... What this draft declaration does is to say that the term 'peoples' as used in the Charter and the Covenants does not include indigenous peoples and in so far as it includes them, it only refers to certain rights and not all the fundamental rights. What this draft declaration does is to say the term 'property' as used in the Charter and the Covenants includes all property except for sub-soil elements. This if adopted, is discrimination at its worst by the very body that is supposed to protect the rights of the indigenous peoples. The words in the Charter and any subsequent declarations,

resolutions or covenants must be given a liberal interpretation and we should not in any subsequent instruments seek to qualify or restrict the ambit of their meaning."[51]

Minerals as Part of Land

The Papua New Guinea Constitution also adopted the principles and rules of the English common law and equity as they existed on the 16th of September 1975, inasmuch as they were not inconsistent with the customary rules of law in Papua New Guinea. The adopted English common law is subsidiary to, and its application subject to, the customary laws of Papua New Guinea.

The common law of England is clear on the definition of *land.* "At common law the owner of the land is entitled to all that lies above and below the surface: *cujus est solum, ejus est usque ad coelu et usque ad inferos.* Minerals are part of the land in which they are situated, [*Wilkinson v. Proud* (1843)][52] and may be dealt with by such methods as are appropriate to land dealings. Thus, a vein of coal is land, unless distinguished from the land by a deed of conveyance.[53] A conveyance of freehold land includes the mines and minerals therein unless expressly excluded or previously reserved: [*Williamson v. Wootton* (1855)[54]]."[55]

The English common law allows considerable fragmentation of interests in land. It is possible to reserve the rights to all or any specified minerals from any disposition of land. Thus the ownership of the minerals may be severed from the ownership of the surface. Each stratum has its own incidence to ownership including mining rights, just like strata titles in buildings: [*Cox v. Glue* (1848)].[56]

In addition, a landowner may dispose of a variety of rights regarding minerals without transferring an entire stratum. Examples include a lease of minerals, a licence to search for minerals not conferring on the licensee any rights to discovered minerals: [*Re Haven Gold Mining Co.* (1882)].[57]

Traditional or indigenous landowners in Papua New Guinea have not conveyed, assigned, transferred or done any act which can be interpreted to amount to a termination of their rights to the sub-soil resources under their land. They have not conveyed their interests in writing or in any other manner either to the state or its predecessor in title (being the government of Australia) so as to justify the declaration of the vesting of ownership of those resources in the state in the mining and petroleum legislations.

Property

In most states in the United States of America, the common law maxim of *cujus est solum* mentioned above is applied not because it was adopted as a rule of law in the United States but because deprivation of property without due process of law is inhibited by the Federal Constitution and many State constitutions.[58] The general rule in the USA is that property rights shall be free of arbitrary government interference. The effect of this guarantee is to inhibit taking one person's property and giving it to another.

The term "property" in the USA is used in its most general sense as embracing everything over which a man may have exclusive control or dominion. It has been held sufficiently broad to embrace all character of vested rights. The vested rights in the USA include all the guaranteed rights and freedoms enshrined in the Constitution of Papua New Guinea. It includes not only title and possession but also the rights of acquisition and control, and the right to make any legitimate use or disposal of the thing owned, such as to pledge it for debt, or to sell or transfer it.

The English common law (after the case of *Mines* in 1568)[59], while recognising the ownership of the proprietor of the soil in respect of most mines and minerals therein, reserved to the sovereign, as an incident to his right of coinage, all deposits of gold and silver even when they are discovered on private land. The monarch, however, had full authority to dispose of any such reserved deposits at his pleasure, and in most of the royal charters under which the eastern part of the United States was settled, the grant of the soil expressly included "all mines" as well as every other thing included or borne in or upon it, reserving as rent only, in the reddendum, one-fifth part of all the gold and silver ore, to be delivered at the pit's mouth, free of charge. How the monarch acquired the title in the first instance to be able to effect the grant of the soil to the settlers is the question being asked by Leroy Little Bear and others today.

Neither gold nor silver are used in Papua New Guinean coinage. This particular section of English common law is therefore not applicable to Papua New Guinea.

Neither Papua nor New Guinea was ever acquired by the British or the Germans by one or the other of the four methods of acquisition of title in international law, as explained at the beginning of this chapter. The customary or indigenous landowners have never transferred or ceded or relinquished their title to land and all that it entails at common law or at international law. They are therefore proprietors of all things beneath the surface of their land.

In India, the legal authorities appear clear. The state cannot under the guise of *"public purpose"* confiscate property of a person for the direct benefit of another person. In *R.K. Kochunni v. States of Madras and Kerala* (1960), the majority of the Supreme Court of India said:

> "We cannot say on the materials placed before us that any public interest will be served by depriving a 'sthanee' of his properties and conferring title in his properties ... on others. Nor is there any evidence that there was a real and genuine grievance in this particular section of the public belonging to 'tarwards' justifying the interference by the State. We cannot on the materials placed before us hold that this reform is in the public interest."[60]

The Supreme Court of India appears in the paragraph quoted above to feel that some public grievance must be established by the state to justify the deprivation. If such is to be applied in Papua New Guinea, then the state must establish through evidence that the public at large (in PNG, this will be the landowners) agree to the deprivation as contained in the mining and petroleum legislations. The onus will have to be on the state to justify the legislations rather than on the landowners to prove prior title.
The Indian Supreme Court further held that:

> "The Act is only a legislative device to take the property of one and to vest it in another without compensation and therefore, on its face stamped with unreasonableness."[61]

The test in Papua New Guinea does not include unreasonableness, however the principle laid down by the Indian Supreme Court is of persuasive value to the Courts of Papua New Guinea. It is evidently clear that the relevant provisions[62] of both mining and petroleum legislations are legislative devices to take the property of the customary or indigenous landowners and vest it in the state for the purpose of further vesting it in a third party, the large mining and petroleum explorers-cum-developers.

As to whether or not mining rights are interests in land, the New Zealand Court of Appeal in *Tainui Madri Trust Board v. A.G.* (1989) held that the definition of coal mining rights in their coal mining legislation as "chattel interests" means chattel interest in land. Justice Cook said:

> "Neither the Treaty of Waitangi (State Enterprises) Act 1988 nor any of the legislation with which it is linked has an express definition of "interest in land". It is an Act designed to safeguard Maori claims, to the Waitangi Tribunal. That purpose must properly be taken into account in interpreting it. Bearing in mind the extensive and valuable rights conferred in respect of land by mining licenses and ancillary licenses, I consider that in the natural and ordinary use of the language they are interests in land within the meaning of the 1988 Act. A decision to the contrary would not be, in my opinion common sense."[63]

Section 53 of the PNG Constitution is designed to protect property owners including those who own land by customary tenure, and can in this context be compared to this section of the Treaty of Waitangi Act.

Mining rights are therefore chattel interests in land. It is plain nonsense to argue that the government can deem itself owner of the chattel interests in land when it is not the owner of the realty or the land itself. You cannot sever one from the other by legislation. To do so will be tantamount to deprivation of property rights. The effect of the mining and petroleum legislations in Papua New Guinea is to sever chattel interests in land by providing that the landowners do not have or possess rights to mine minerals on or under their land or to deal in any manner with such minerals.

A similar idea was expressed by Justice Buckley with reference to certain compulsory licensing and compensation legislation in the English case of *Re Associated Portland Cement Manufacturers Ltd's Application* (1965) when he said:

> "The applicants have at present no title to or interest in any of the brick earth on the site. What they are seeking is the right to go on to the site to win and remove the brick earth there. This is a property right of a kind which has been well known for centuries under the name of 'profit a prendre'. Such a right may at common law be granted in perpetuity or for a limited term; but where the profit is the right to remove minerals from the soil of the servient tenement, it

involved the right for the grantee to acquire the ownership of part of the grantor's freehold even though the right of working may be for a limited period only. It is not true to say that in the present case the grant of the right which the applicant seeks will only deprive the respondents of the opportunity for a while to use parts of the surface of their land for agricultural purposes: they will, by the extraction of the brick earth, be permanently deprived of a part of their existing freehold which represents part of the value of that capital asset ..."[64]

The scheme of the mining and petroleum legislations in Papua New Guinea is to not only temporarily deprive the landowners of the opportunity to use parts of their traditional land for any purpose they see fit but to also deprive them permanently of a part of their existing traditional land, that is, the gold and the minerals forming part of the land under the surface of that land. This in most cases represents 99.99% of the value of their land.

To apply the reasoning that mining rights are chattel interests in land in Papua New Guinea, would require the state or the mining companies to acquire part of the traditional land from the owners. Such land can only be acquired for valuable consideration. How does one determine the value of that consideration? Obviously, the value of the gold and minerals or other resources therein form part of the value of the land. The existing practice is to determine the value based on the value of the trees and other improvements on the surface of the land.[65] This practice is in contradiction to the English common law rule that the resources form part of the land and should be taken into account in its valuation.[66]

VIII Conclusion

I have attempted to show that, whichever law is applied in Papua New Guinea, the result will be the same. International law supports the indigenous landowners. Constitutional law supports the landowners. The precedents of Commonwealth countries supports the landowners. United States rules of law supports the landowners. Above all else the common law of England as is adopted in Papua New Guinea on 16th December 1975 supports the landowners' claim to their wealth and resources.

I have been brief and selective in the authorities cited or referred to.

The bibliography sets out in full the authorities and materials I have had the pleasure of being influenced by in writing the book.

I hope this book will convince the mining industry and the officials of the government of Papua New Guinea that they are defending a system which is contrary to international and domestic law and which, if not changed, will not receive the support of domestic and world opinion in years to come. I hope also that this book will broaden the knowledge of the members of the press corps who have written disparaging commentary against the interests of the landowners in Papua New Guinea. It should also serve as a good reference book for those who are intent on protecting and promoting indigenous rights to property.

My statements at the United Nations which are reproduced in part here go towards establishing the case at international law for the rights of indigenous peoples everywhere.[67] My statement to the visiting members of the Australia Papua New Guinea Business Council in 1990 warned about the seige mentality at work at different levels of society.[68] Whilst the mining industry and the government feels an increased sense of seige by uncontrolled actions of the indigenous landowners either demanding compensation or destroying capital items at mining sites, it should be stressed that the landowners also feel a sense of seige that the government which is supposed to protect their land rights and rights to sub-surface resources has taken the side of the multinationals and is depriving them of their constitutionally guaranteed rights as well as rights at international law.

The solution can be found in the words of Paul Ehrlich, on the treatment of cancer:

> "A cancer is an uncontrolled multiplication of cells; ... treating only the symptoms of cancer may make the victim more comfortable at first, but eventually he dies – often horribly ... We must shift our efforts from treatment of symptoms to the cutting out of the cancer. The operation will demand many apparently brutal and heartless decisions. The pain may be intense. But the disease is so far advanced that only with radical surgery does the patient have a chance of survival."[69]

The mining companies in Papua New Guinea have called on the government to establish elite law enforcement squads to deal with what they claim to be "terrorist" activities of the landowners. The Australian government has agreed to provide "boomerang" aid for the training of this elite squad. Will the government of Papua New Guinea, supported by the mining companies and aided by the Australian government, be treating the symptoms or will it be establishing a foundation for radical surgery. Currently, it appears radical surgery is being undertaken on the island of Bougainville, where many people on both sides have been killed.

"Lack of political will" is a phrase which has been said to describe the inaction of any government on any issue. Yet do we really know what is meant by that phrase? It can be used to describe a situation where the rich and powerful failed to act against their own interests. Political will is a way of averting the eyes from the ugly facts. Political will stops short of asking who gains and who loses what, when, where and how. Robert Chambers, in describing these factors, said:

> "Many outsiders prefer diagnosis and prescriptions which gratify them. The most immediately gratifying are those where direct action yields quick results against visible physical weakness ... Outsiders also prefer diagnosis and prescriptions from which they and those like them will gain and not lose."[70]

He argued that the poor are in a deprivation trap from which they cannot get out. He identified the clusters of rural households as follows:
a   The household is poor;
b   The household is physically weak;
c   The household is isolated;
d   The household is vulnerable; and
e   The household is powerless.

Chambers argued that linking the five clusters gives twenty possible causal relations, which in their negative forms interlock like a web to trap people in their deprivation. The strength of these linkages varies and poverty is a strong determinant of the others. The physical weakness of the household contributes to poverty. Isolation (lack of education, remoteness, being out of contact) sustains poverty. Vulnerability is part of the many links. Powerlessness which includes ignorance of the law or unavailability of legal advise and services, contributes to poverty in many ways, not least through exploitation by the powerful.

In Papua New Guinea, *the powerful* is the government and the multinationals and the people who represent their interests and the so-called principle of market forces. In a largely uneducated, traditional and pluralistic society such as Papua New Guinea, unless the government takes a decisive step to check its intimacy with western oriented philosophies and give effective political and legislative recognition to the existence of the fundamental, inherent and time immemorial rights of its diverse peoples, the thinly veiled thread that is currently holding the country together will wither and tear to the detriment of all concerned.

It is time for change so that the fiction of Crown right and eminent domain created by the *"unprincipled white men"*[72] to perpetuate and legalise daylight robbery should not be maintained to defeat our God-given inheritance.

Part B
Equality and participation

Equality and participation

1 Introduction

The Constitution of Papua New Guinea has specified the National Goals and Directive Principles which are meant to guide our political leaders in decision making for the benefit of the people. Whether foreign ideologies which will affect the political, economic, social, religious and cultural life of the country can be imported is questionable. There are diverse ways of importing such foreign concepts. For instance the cultural life of the country can be affected and changed by continuous mass media publication through radio, television, newspapers, periodicals and books. Political ideologies can be propagated through the education process, either by utilisation of the freedom of the press or by classroom education.[1]

The economic influences take the form of superimposed business methods and the creation of the tools of doing business. One of these tools is the creation of the so-called landowner companies, a fiction created by foreign accountants and supported by foreign law firms as a substitute for clan participation in business activities. Despite the fact that the clan, in traditional culture, transcends realms beyond the understanding of these agents of capitalism, the agents are not prepared to give corporate legal recognition to the clan structures[2] even though these have existed in Papua New Guinea for many thousands of years. The business people insisted on introducing the structures they knew best – the corporate entities pursuant to their company laws. They then created companies to represent the interests of landowners – companies managed sometimes by themselves or their agents at exorbitant fees and supported by cronies as trustee directors representing the interests of the landowners. The trustees are not necessarily chosen in accordance with local custom and in most cases they are not traditional chiefs. A breakdown of communications between the chiefs, who by custom control all land for and on behalf of the clan members, and the trustees who have no leadership rights by custom, ensues. The stage is now set for applying the divide and rule theory in practice. Under such circumstances it is very unlikely that the traditional chief will be able to maintain a sense of order and balance in the society. Not only has he lost face, his power of control over the land has been taken away from him. He is powerless to defend himself, his rights and the rights of the other members of the clan who may not be willing to support the trustees. The foreigner is now effectively in control of the situation. If the chief complains, the foreigner will call in the police and argue that the trustees are the true owners of the land and must be protected against the unscrupulous fortune seeking carpetbaggers. If the chief and his supporters use physical violence to protect their rights, they will be branded as "terrorists".[3] If the going gets too tough for the foreigner, he will pack his bags and leave the country. Meanwhile, the problem he helped create is used abroad as evidence of instability. Financiers react by demanding huge insurance premiums for investors wishing to undertake future projects in the country.

The complete disregard of the clan system and the non-recognition of the authority of the clan Chiefs will result in significant economic disaggregation and future social upheavals.[4] This disregard and non-recognition, it can be argued, led to the closure of CRA's Bougainville mine in 1989 following the problems with landowners. The stage has been created by CRA also in respect to the Mt. Kare Alluvial mine.[5] Included in the Court documents filed in Court by some disgruntled landowners were claims of bribery and corruption (including allegations of wining, dining and womanising after being flown to Australia) against certain agents of CRA. Now CRA has decided to withdraw from the project but reserves it's rights to the hard-ore deposits, forced to do so after sustaining several million dollars worth of damages to capital items including the destruction of a helicopter. One would think CRA would have learnt its lesson from the Bougainville precedent. CRA is still involved in two other possible gold mines in the country. It is hoped their *modus operandi* is not repeated in those areas as well. Other companies must take heed of these lessons and avoid a repetition of that precedent.

In the meantime the government and the country continues to get the thumbs down in the Australian financial markets as the ideal country for investment and for conducting mining and petroleum exploration activities.[6] This does not seem to deter companies from countries other then

Australia, notably from South East Asian and European countries and the United States.[7] Given this situation, one must come to the conclusion that it must be the attitude of Australians doing business in Papua New Guinea that has created all these problems and not the government and people of Papua New Guinea. Generally, multinational companies are used to doing business in different countries which sometimes have vastly different regimes. They are therefore more tolerant towards the rights of the receiving state and the expectations of the people of that state. Australian companies and their managers however have not had that vast experience and are therefore limited in their experience to Papua New Guinea and Australia. Accordingly, the attitude of their managers, sometimes bordering on colonialism, has not changed and they continue to treat Papua New Guinea as if it is their backyard rather then another independent country with its own government and style of doing business. They insisted on the application of the Australian laws and standards when they should know that such legislations and standards may not be suitable to the country.

The founding fathers of the Papua New Guinea Constitution wrote in their report:

> "Countries of the third world have become increasingly concerned by, and resentful of, the extent to which giant foreign corporations are dominating their economies and obtaining massive profits from operations in their countries. This situation was clearly evidenced at a recent Special Meeting of the United Nations to consider the need to drastically change the present International Economic Order. We in Papua New Guinea are all too familiar with the extent and effect of the present foreign control of our economy ... Our own people are, however, more fortunate then those in many other new states in that most still have their own land, their rights to which they rightly intend to protect most vigorously."[8]

If the landowners were to take up arms to protect their land and all that it entails, would it not be in pursuit of that right which the founding fathers of the Constitution had so rightly recognised?

While not much had taken place about the change in the international economic order – it had changed for the worse as the commodity prices are at an all time low – domestically, in Papua New Guinea people are demanding a greater participation in the fruits of the exploitation of its resources. The question being asked at all levels is what sort of participation is acceptable. Some Papua New Guineans want participation at the spin-off levels of major projects, in trucking, construction, wholesaling and retailing businesses etc. Others are not satisfied with such spin-off businesses which are clearly aimed at seducing the immediate landowners into agreeing to the development project. It has no bearing on the other Papua New Guineans not directly affected by the project. Other Papua New Guineans must also be made beneficiaries of such projects. Their involvement can only be effected by way of equity participation. Should they therefore be prohibited from such participation? The Constitution provides that:

> "We declare our second goal to be for all citizens to have an equal opportunity to participate in, and benefit from, the development of our country."[9]

The Constitution further calls for the "maximisation of the number of citizens participating in every aspect of development".[10]

It is clear from these passages that the government must give priority to any development proposals which will involve the maximisation of participation by the citizens of the country as opposed to the interests of the foreign multinationals which may deny such participation. When the Constitution called for participation in "every aspect of development", it did not limit that participation to spin-off activities only. The words "every aspect" must be read liberally so as to include "ownership" of certain aspects of the development projects including equity participation.

It is also abundantly clear that participation is meant for citizens and is not to be limited to government participation on behalf of its citizens.

11 Monticello proposal

When oil was discovered in the highlands of Papua New Guinea, the operator of the field, Chevron Corporation of United States, proposed to the government that it would apply for a development licence as well as the pipeline licence to pipe the oil from the field to an off-shore floating and export terminal some 250 kilometres away in the Gulf of Papua. A group of Papua New Guineans including myself formed a company called Monticello Enterprises Pty Limited to which we became the principals. The company commissioned an international financial institution, Schroeders Australia, to put together a financial package and a submission to the government of Papua New Guinea for a pipeline licence to be granted to an independent Papua New Guinea publicly owned company. The Monticello proposal, as it became known in the industry, created a stir in political and industrial circles in Papua New Guinea, Australia and United States. The motives of the principals of Monticello were questioned and threats were issued to the continued viability of the business interests of each of the principals of Monticello. One was threatened with termination of employment if his continued involvement resulted in Chevron's cancellation of its lease of an office space in Port Moresby.[11] Another, who owned a substantial interest in a computer company, had the proposed contract to supply computers to Chevron threatened with cancellation if he persisted.[12] The third, who was in the process of establishing his company in the tankship business, was informed of the possibility of not winning contracts to carry oil in the event of his persistence.[13]

I found myself in a situation where, having already strained the relations with my partners in my legal firm[14] following the publication of my article on ownership of resources in Papua New Guinea in *The Times* newspaper of Papua New Guinea, in which I espoused the theory of ownership by landowners as opposed to the state, there was no other option but to agree to a dissolution of the partnership practice. My former and now late partner Thomas Leslie Reiner had acted for many mining and petroleum companies. The power of the corporate relationship with business houses in Port Moresby was stretched at all levels to stifle the Monticello proposal. Our own businesses depended on the goodwill of Chevron and other large business houses in Port Moresby for our continued survival. We could not fight that powerful force unless the government was with us.

In putting together the proposal we had gone to the Prime Minister (who was then the Right Honorable Rabbie Namaliu) and sought from him an understanding that he will support us in our endeavours. He agreed subject to its financial feasibility. Based on that understanding we commissioned and paid for the preparation of the project proposal which was submitted to the government. We were assured by Schroeders Australia that once the pipeline licence was issued there would be no problems in securing funds for the construction of the pipeline and that they would assist in securing the required funds. They considered the project to be low risk, as it was a utility project and its utilisation was guaranteed.

The proposal to the government, which received a lot of publicity in the local press, was presented at about the time of the appointment of the new American Ambassador to Papua New Guinea[15]. It also coincided with the visit to Washington by the then Prime Minister Rabbie Namaliu. On the Ambassador's arrival in Port Moresby, the Australian High Commissioner[16] to Papua New Guinea invited Sir Mekere Morauta (also a principal of Monticello), Lady Morauta, my wife and myself to dinner at his residence to meet with the new United States Ambassador. Towards the end of dinner the Ambassador, who was seated at one end of the table with our respective wives, began boasting about the fact that the Monticello proposal would not be entertained by the Prime Minister and the government because President Bush had put the right words in the ears of Prime Minister Namaliu during his visit to Washington.

I felt at that time that the Ambassador had not recognised our names in the newspaper articles that week and did not associate us with the Monticello proposal. He may, however, have made that association and had deliberately let it out of the bag to show how powerful Chevron was in being able to get the President of the United States to intervene on its behalf. Nevertheless, the Australian High Commissioner was tactful and diplomatic and immediately suggested we retire for coffee in the adjoining room to diffuse a somewhat tense situation. Over coffee the American Ambassador's wife asked me my employment status to which I responded that I was a villager with no fixed employment or abode, as I commute between my village[17] and Port Moresby. I think she believed me.

Until today I still want to know what President Bush said to Namaliu to convince him to change his mind about his political resolve to support our proposal. Of all the Prime Ministers that Papua New Guinea has ever had, I will grant Namaliu ten out of ten for not having the political will to do anything worthwhile for history to remember him by. A friend of mine aptly characterised him as an emperor without a robe.[18] He epitomises the saying that lack of political will is where the rich and powerful failed to act against their own interests. To put it another way, he exercised political will by averting his eyes from the ugly facts. He failed to give credence to the national goal of equal opportunity and participation by Papua New Guinea citizens.

III Conclusion

The briefing paper to the government on the Monticello proposal, John Millet's commentary on its effect on investor's confidence and participation by Papua New Guineans, Joe Tauvasa's article on economic nationalism and Sir Mekere's commentary are in the appendices of this book. It should be pointed out that the Institute of National Affairs in Papua New Guinea is funded by foreign capital and serves as the think-tank for pooling ideas before submitting them to the government. It represents foreign interests and not national interests as the name suggests. It serves as a powerful tool for influencing decision making at the government level without invoking the wrath of the government against each individual company or an executive of a company. To that extent it provides a shield for foreign companies.

The mining and petroleum companies operate through the Chamber of Mines and Petroleum, the current Executive Director of which was the former Chief Government Geologist (a non-national)[19] and in that capacity was an influential member of the Mining and Petroleum Advisory Board which advises the Minister on any proposals by members of the Chamber. He left the government and immediately joined the Chamber. A Papua New Guinean leader who is subject to the Leadership Code is prohibited from taking this course for at least a period of three years.[20] Unfortunately, the Leadership Code does not apply to foreigners who hold influential middle management positions in government. The Chamber provides a shield for influencing decision making at government level. The founding fathers of our Constitution warned us against the influence of these companies in the following terms:

> "We must avoid a situation where foreign capital controls the destiny of our people."[21]
> "It is essential that we be highly selective as to the type of enterprise we allow into the country ... We must not allow any foreign enterprise into the country unless we can be sure that it will abide by our laws, and will not make any attempt to interfere with our political and civic affairs."[22]
> "All of us should be aware that we are trustees for future generations of our people and have the fundamental duty of protecting the interests of our country by ensuring that its sovereignty and

independence are not undermined by foreign interests. We need to appreciate that the danger to our national integrity is less likely to come from military action than from economic dominance which stems partly from our colonial heritage and partly from our acceptance of too many large, highly capitalised foreign enterprises which appear to bring us attractive material benefits, but in reality exploit our resources for their own benefit, undermine our self confidence, and make us increasingly dependent on foreign capital, and foreign technical and managerial skills ..."[23]

"Only if the great majority of our people become fully aware of the implications for their children and grandchildren of the operation of these massive foreign enterprises – the rapid breakdown of traditional societies, their values and customs; the encouragement of an attitude of dependence instead of one of self-reliance; the irreparable damage which these enterprises can cause to the environment – will we be able to adequately protect ourselves from the old colonial and neo-colonial policy of 'divide and rule', which is often used by these enterprises to achieve their ends."[24]

Is it not possible to consider the formation of the Institute for National Affairs and the Chamber of Mines and Petroleum as organisations primarily to represent foreign capital in effecting change in our political and civic affairs? If so, we have failed to honour the wisdom of the founding fathers of our Constitution. The current Prime Minister, the Right Honorable Paias Wingti, has stated[25] that if he had been in government he would have had the political resolve to cause the grant of the pipeline licence to a Papua New Guinean publicly owned company as proposed by Monticello. He is now in government and I truly hope that he will have the political will not to avert his eyes from the ugly facts and to give due recognisance to economic nationalism and greater Papua New Guinean participation in all major projects. He has taken decisive action against the rebels on Bougainville at the behest of the Bougainville Council of Chiefs. He has insisted on a review upwards of the government's equity participation in the Porgera Gold Mine project[26] from the current 10 percent and has succeeded in obtaining approval from the other joint venture partners to divest a part of their percentage interests in the mine. This has resulted in an increase of the state's interest to 25 percent. Unlike his predecessor, here is an emperor who has already donned a cloak. At the end of his term we will need to determine the colour(s) of that cloak.

The Peruvian economist, Hernando de Soto[27] aptly described the problems of bringing developing countries into the market economy. The problem, he says, is not the desire of the governments of developing countries to convert their thinking and policies. Nearly all of them are already signatories of, or parties to, the UN Declarations on Human Rights, which recognise property rights as fundamental. In Papua New Guinea, numerous political statements have been made by politicians both in government and in the opposition recognising the rights of landowners. Hernando de Soto highlighted the problem of developing countries as follows:

> "It is law that defines the relationship of ownership rights to people. Property is a collection of rights defined by law which makes no sense outside it. People do not own a parcel of land, or a real estate unit, but rather what they have are certain rights over the property – to buy, to sell, to mortgage – which are recognised by law. Indeed the governance of a market system is essentially legal: corporations, limited liability, contracts and an inadequate business environment are impossible outside the law ...
>
> "When I was growing up in Peru, I was told that the farms I visited belonged to farming communities and not to the individual farmers. Yet as I walked from field to field, a different dog would bark. The dogs were ignorant of the prevailing law; all they know was which land their masters controlled. In the next 150 years those nations whose laws recognise what dogs already know will be the ones who enjoy the benefits of a modern market economy."[28]

The Peruvian dogs must have gone to the same school as the Papua New Guinean dogs. Shall the Papua New Guinean politicians have the will and the creativity to throw away the shackles of Australian laws and practices and embark on a new road to formalise in legal documents what the dogs already know?

Part C
Appendices

Appendix 1

Commodore Erskine's Proclamation over Papua of 1884[1]

Proclamation on behalf of Her most gracious Majesty Victoria, by the grace of God, of the United Kingdom of Great Britain and Ireland, Queen, Defender of the Faith, Empress of India, establishing a Protectorate of Her most gracious Majesty over a portion of New Guinea and the islands adjacent thereto.

To all to whom these present shall come. Greeting.

Whereas it has become essential for the protection of the lives and properties of the native inhabitants of New Guinea, and for the purpose of preventing the occupation of portions of that country by persons whose proceedings, unsanctioned by any lawful authority, might tend to injustice, strife, and bloodshed, and who, under the pretence of legitimate trade and intercourse, might endanger the liberties and possess themselves of the lands of such native inhabitants, that a British Protectorate should be established over a certain portion of such country and the islands adjacent thereto.

And whereas Her Majesty, having taken into Her gracious consideration the urgent necessity of Her protection to such inhabitants, has directed me to proclaim such protection in a formal manner at this place: Now I, James Elphinstone Erskine, Captain in the Royal Navy and Commodore of the Australian station, one of Her Majesty's Naval Aides-de-Camp, do hereby, in the name of Her most gracious Majesty, declare and proclaim the establishment of such Protectorate over such portions of the coast and the adjacent islands as is more particularly described in the Schedule hereunto annexed.

And I hereby proclaim and declare that no acquisition of land whensoever or howsoever acquired within the limits of the protectorate hereby established will be recognised by Her Majesty. And I do hereby, on behalf of Her Majesty, command and enjoin all persons whom it may concern, to take notice of this proclamation.

Schedule
All that portion of the southern shores of New Guinea commencing from the boundary of that portion of the country claimed by the government of the Netherlands on the 141st meridian of east longitude to East Cape, with all islands adjacent thereto south of East Cape to Kosman Island, inclusive, together with the islands in the Goschen Straits.

Given at the harbour of Port Moresby on the 6th day of November 1884.
(Signed) *James E. Erskine*, Commodore.
God Save the Queen!

Commodore Erskine's Speech to the Assembled People
Commodore Erskine then made a speech to the assembled people:

> "I desire on behalf of Her Majesty the Queen, to explain to you the meaning of the Ceremonial which you have just witnessed. It is a Proclamation that from this time forth you are placed under the protection of Her Majesty's Government, that evil-disposed men will not be permitted to occupy your Country, to seize your lands, or to take you away from your own homes. I have been instructed to say to you that what you have seen done here today is to give you the strongest assurance of Her Majesty's gracious protection of you, and to warn bad evil-disposed men that if they attempt to do you harm they will be promptly punished by the Officers of the Queen. Your lands will be secured to you. Your wives and children will be protected.
>
> "Should any injury be done to you, you will immediately inform Her Majesty's Officers who will reside amongst you, and they will hear your complaints and do justice. You will look upon all white persons whom the Queen permits to reside amongst you as your friends and Her Majesty's subjects. The Queen will permit nobody to reside here

who does you injury. You will under no circumstances inflict punishment yourselves upon any white person; but if such person has done you wrong, you will tell Her Majesty's Officers of the wrong, in order that the case be fairly inquired into. You must know that it is for your protection and security and to prevent bloodshed that the Queen sends me here to you, and will send Her Officers to live amongst you. And now I hope that you all clearly understand that we are here as your friends. You will all keep peace amongst yourselves, and if you have disputes with each other you will bring them before the Queen's Officers, who will settle them for you without bloodshed.

"Should bad men come amongst you, bringing fire-arms and gunpowder and intoxicating liquors, you are not to buy them; and are to give notice at once to the Queen's Officers, so that such men may be punished. Always keep in your minds that the Queen guards and watches over you, looks upon you as Her children, and will not allow anyone to harm you, and will soon send Her trusted Officers to carry out Her gracious intentions in the establishment of this Protectorate.

"This interesting and important ceremony being now formally concluded, it only remains for me, in Her Majesty's name to express the fervent hope that, under the blessing of Almighty God, the establishment of this Portectorate may conduce to the peace, happiness, and welfare of the people of this vast Territory.

"May the British flag, which we have this day planted on these shores, be to the people of this portion of New Guinea the symbol of their freedom – their liberty; and their rights and privileges. May it be to them a Protectorate in deed as well as in name, protecting them alike from the encroachments of foreigners and the aggressive or unlawful actions of persons of whatever nationality. May the Blessings of civilisation and Christianity, the seeds of which have been already sown by English hands, in the persons of the good and valiant gentlemen who I am delighted to see present on this occasion, increase and multiply exeedingly amongst them; and, lastly as the Union Jack which has on several former occasions been hoisted on the shores of New Guinea and the adjacent islands, is on this day for the first time displayed and hoisted on New Guinea, under the authority and by the command of Her Most Gracious Majesty Queen Victoria, I most fervently pray that the establishment of a British Protectorate on these shores may tend to ensure the integrity and inviolability of the great Australian Colonies, and may promote the best interests of their people; and I trust that this important step may be attended with the happiest results, and rebound to the honour of Her Most Gracious Majesty the Queen, for whom I now invite you to give three hearty cheers."

Note appendix 1

1   (When this Proclamation was published as a supplement to the *Queensland Government Gazette* on 23 December 1884, the D'Entrecasteaux Group of islands were added to the Schedule.) Great Britain, House of Commons, Sessional Papers, Vol. LIV (1884-5), C.-4217, Encl. 1 in No. 148, p. 122. Reproduced here from documents maintained by the University of Papua New Guinea, History of Papua New Guinea, New Guinea Collection Section (06.102).

Appendix 2

Imperial Charter for the Neu Guinea Kompagnie of 17th May 1885[1]

We, Wilhelm, by the Grace of God German Emperor, King of Prussia, etc. make known and proclaim as follows:

Whereas, in August 1884, we promised our protection to a group of German subjects, which since then has adopted the name of Neu Guinea Kompagnie, for a colonial enterprise initiated by them in certain island districts in the Western part of the Pacific which are not under the sovereignty of any other power;

Whereas this Company, under the control of our Commissioner, by an expedition which it fitted out for itself, has acquired and taken into possession in these districts, harbours and sections of the coast for the purpose of cultivation and the establishment of trading stations, which, on our instruction, were subsequently placed under our protection by our warships;

Whereas the two German trading firms which had previously established trading stations and acquired land in parts of these districts have joined the Company;

And whereas the Company, legally represented by our Privy Councillor for Commerce, Adolph von Hansemann, has now declared that it undertakes to create and maintain in the Protectorate at its own expense such administrative institutions as will serve the promotion of trade and the economic utilisation of the land as well as the establishment and strengthening of peaceful relations with the natives and their civilisation, at the same time requesting that in order to achieve these aims it be granted by means of an Imperial Charter the right to exercise local sovereignty under our sovereignty and, in addition, the exclusive right to occupy and to dispose of ownerless land and to conclude contracts regarding land and land rights with the natives, under the supervision of our Government;

We now grant the Neu Guinea Kompagnie this our Imperial Charter and confirm hereby that we have assumed sovereignty over the districts in question.

These districts are:
1. That part of the mainland of New Guinea which is not under British or Dutch sovereignty. This district, which, on application of the Company, we have permitted to be called 'Kaiser Wilhelms-Land', extends along the island's north-east coast from the 141st degree of east longitude (Greenwich) to a point near Mitre Rock where the 8th degree of south latitude intersects the coast, and is bounded to the south and west by a line which follows the 8th degree of south latitude to the point where it is intersected by the 147th degree of east longitude, runs from there straight in a north-westerly direction to the intersection of the 6th degree of south latitude and the 144th degree of east longitude, from there further in a west-north-westerly direction to the intersection of the 5th degree of south latitude and the 141st degree of east longitude and then follows this meridian north to the sea.
2. The islands lying of the coast of this part of New Guinea as well as the islands of the Archipelago, which so far has been called that of New Britain and which, on application of the Company, and with our authorisation, shall bear the name 'Bismarck-Archipelago', and all other islands situated north-east of New Guinea between the equator and the 8th degree of south latitude and between the 141st and 154th degree of east longitude.

We also herewith grant the said Company, in return for its undertaking to create and maintain the administrative institutions for which it has taken responsibility and to bear the costs of an adequate administration of justice, the corresponding rights of local sovereignty as well as the exclusive right to occupy and to dispose of ownerless land in the Protectorate and to conclude contracts regarding land and land rights with the natives, all this under the supervision of our Government which will enact those regulations necessary to protect the natives and to preserve rights of ownership, which were duly acquired at an earlier date.

We reserve to our Government the organisation of the administration of justice, as well as the regulation and the conduct of relations between the Protectorate and foreign Governments.

We hereby promise and order that all our officials and officers shall, by protecting and supporting the Company and its officials in all lawful undertakings, carry this our Charter into effect.

This our Imperial Charter we grant to the Neu Guinea Kompagnie on condition that it will complete its legal organisation according to the German laws at the latest within one year from the present day, that the members of its Board of Directors, or any other persons entrusted with directing its affairs, are subjects of the German Reich, and subject to future amendments of this our Charter and the regulations enacted by our Government in its implementation as well as to any further instructions to be issued in exercise of our supreme sovereignty over the Protectorate, and which the Company must observe under pain of forfeiting its claim to our protection.

In witness thereof we have executed this our Charter with our own hand and caused to be attached to it our Imperial Seal.

Given at Berlin, 17th May 1885.
Wilhelm Furst v. Bismarck

Note appendix 2
1   Reproduced from *The Land Law of German New Guinea, A Collection of Documents* by Peter and Bridget Sack, ANU, Canberra, 1975; D.K.G., Vol. 1, 434-6.

Appendix 3

Contract between the Reich and the Neu Guinea Kompagnie of 7th October 1898[1]

The following contract is made between the Chancellor of the Reich on behalf of the Reich and the Neu Guinea Kompagnie, represented by its Board of Directors:

Clause 1
The Reich resumes and shall itself exercise the local sovereignty granted to the Neu Guinea Kompagnie by the Imperial Charters of 17th May 1885 and 13th December 1886, as well as by subsequent Imperial Ordinances, over the Protectorate in the Pacific described therein, including all rights and duties appertaining thereto.

Clause 2
The Neu Guinea Kompagnie renounces in favour of the Reich the special property rights for the whole area of the Protectorate described in Clause 1 which were granted to it by the Charters and which it possesses by virtue of the same, to wit:
a the exclusive right to occupy and to dispose of ownerless land, as well as to conclude contracts with the natives regarding land and land rights,
b the right to make the following commercial undertakings dependent on its permission and subject to certain conditions, in particular the payment of fees: fishing for pearl-shell, pearls and trepang, exploiting deposits of guano or other fertilisers, mining for ores, precious stones and combustible minerals, exploiting coconut groves, not in the possession of natives or otherwise privately owned, for copra, coastal fish-

ing and felling timber for commercial or trading purposes in all areas which are not privately owned.

Clause 3
The Neu Guinea Kompagnie cedes to the Reich free of charge the buildings, inventory items, harbour and shipping installations, vessels and movables used in administering the country, as shown in the attached list, in the condition in which they are at the time of the transfer. In addition to the buildings the blocks of land on which they are erected will be transferred, as well as those blocks which through their use as gardens or for other domestic purposes are attached to them. Likewise all blocks used by the New Guinea Kompagnie as public roads or for other public purposes shall be transferred to the Reich.

Clause 4
The Neu Guinea Kompagnie will oblige the officials employed by it in the Protectorate to take over any official duties connected with the local administration, such as the duties of police, postal, or harbour officials, court clerks, customs or tax collectors etc., in all places where no suitable Imperial officials are posted, without compensation for the personal effort involved, in so far as this is at all compatible wth the duties they have to perform in the service of the Company.

The transfer of such official duties is to be preceded by an agreement with the Company's highest representative in the Protectorate; the recall of such an official on the part of the Company is to be preceded by an announcement at the earliest possible date.

The Neu Guinea Kompagnie will also make available for administrative purposes the use of its steamships serving the Protectorate, be it by way of charter for a certain time or be it for payment of personal fares and freight expenses on the ships' regular runs, both at appropriate rates, and will comply with the needs of the Administration as far as possible.

The mutual use of existing hospitals by officials and labourers, as well as the mutual granting of medical assistance shall be made as easy as possible by both parties, and the conditions for this shall be settled by special agreement.

Clause 5
By virtue of the Ordinance of 1st August 1894 the Neu Guinea Kompagnie

has up to date minted 50,000 New Guinea marks in gold, 200,035 New Guinea marks in silver and 20,000 New Guinea marks in bronze or copper coins. The Company renounces the right to any further minting. The Reich reserves the right to withdraw the New Guinea coins after a certain redemption period. In this case the Neu Guinea Kompagnie is obliged to exchange the coins for an equal amount of Reich coins. If the exchange of New Guinea coins for Reich coins is not carried out by the Reich, it will refund to the Neu Guinea Kompagnie the expenses, which the latter incurs through the transport of withdrawn coins to Berlin and the return consignment of the same amount in Reich coins.

If the period of redemption expires before 1st April 1905, half of the amount received during this time shall be withdrawn at the expense of the Reich.

Until the expiry of the redemption period it shall continue to be the Neu Guinea Kompagnie's duty to write cheques for the delivery of New Guinea coins in accordance with Section 4 of its Ordinance Regarding the Minting of New Guinea Coins, of 1st August 1894.

Clause 6

The Reich grants the Neu Guinea Kompagnie a capital of 4,000,000 marks with the right to pay the same in ten yearly instalments of 400,000 marks each, which fall due on 1st April each year, beginning with 1st April 1899, without paying interest on the remaining amount.

The Neu Guinea Kompagnie is obliged to spend each instalment within four years on commercial undertakings in the interest of the Protectorate and has to account for the amount spent during each financial year by presenting an annual balance to the Chancellor of the Reich or a Commissioner appointed by him.

In order to ensure the functioning of these commercial undertakings, depending on local labour as they do, measures will be taken within the above period to make it easier for the Neu Guinea Kompagnie to recruit natives in Kaiser Wilhelmsland under the supervision of the Government.

Clause 7[2]

The Neu Guinea Kompagnie is also entitled to take into possession, without payment to the Reich, 50,000 hectares of land of its choice in Kaiser Wilhelmsland and the islands belonging thereto within three years from 1st April 1899 – without prejudice to duly acquired rights of third parties –

with the proviso, however, that the selection of land along the coast and river banks on the two main islands named above[3] is limited to a total sea- and river- frontage of 100 kilometres. The land to be selected along the sea or rivers must extend at least one kilometre inland, unless the natural topography of the area in question makes an adjustment necessary. Land thus acquired is subject to the provisions of an expropriation ordinance to be enacted regarding the transfer of land for public purposes. The Neu Guinea Kompagnie is obliged to inform the representative of the Reich in the Protectorate in each case of the land it has selected and to prove within one year that the selected land was, in accordance with existing laws, either occupied as ownerless or acquired from natives.

Further, the Neu Guinea Kompagnie has equipped at its own expense an expedition with the object of exploring the Ramu River and opening up the Bismarck Range as well as establishing stations for these purposes. In recognition thereof provision will be made to guarantee to the Company the exclusive right to exploit the area of the Ramu River, lying between the 5th degree of south latitude and its watershed, for precious metals and combustible minerals. The Company is to pay the Reich a fee of ten percent of the income derived from this exploitation after all expenses have been paid. Instead of receiving this fee the Reich is also free at the beginning of each new financial year to participate in the mining operations of the Company in the said area in such a way that profits and expenses are equally shared.

Clause 8
Subject to the approval of the Federal Council and Parliament this agreement becomes effective on 1st April 1899.

If, by mutual agreement, the Reich takes over officials from the service of the Company, the Neu Guinea Kompagnie will bear the expenses of their journey to the Protectorate and the Reich the cost of their subsequent return journey.

Taxes and other duties which are payable for certain period in advance are to be shared proportionately for the period involved.

Any credited customs and other duties which were due before the 1st April 1899, as well as heirless estates for which proceedings have already been commenced, remain the property of the Neu Guinea Kompagnie.

For fees payable in accordance with the Order regarding the Ground Book[4] the decisive date is that on which the registration of ownership or any other judicial act took place and not the date of which the memorandum of fees was served. If the Neu Guinea Kompagnie incurred expenses in Ground Book matters instituted before 1st April 1899, which are to be refunded by the applicant, the amounts paid are due to the New Guinea Kompagnie. The same applies to survey fees which were due before 1st April 1899 in respect of surveys carried out at the request of private persons by the surveyor in the service of the Neu Guinea Kompagnie.

In addition the Neu Guinea Kompagnie retains all it has acquired or levied in the actual exercise of its rights and privileges before the 1st April 1899, including claims to land for which it possesses acquisition titles, although no application for registration has so far been made, but subject to an examination of the title by the Ground Book Office.

The option for 400 hectares of land on Weber Harbour in the Gazelle Peninsula which the Neu Guinea Kompagnie has contractually granted to the Catholic Mission of the Sacred Heart of Jesus is also to remain for the latter in force in relation to the Reich.

Executed in duplicate, Berlin, 7th October, 1898

The Chancellor of the Reich Neu Guinea Kompagnie
(signed) *Furst zu Hohenlohe* (signed) *A.v. Hansemann*
 Chairman of the Board of Directors

 (signed) *E. Russell*
 Member of the Board of Directors

Notes appendix 3
1 Reproduced from *The Land Law of German New Guinea, A Collection of Documents* by Peter and Bridget Sack, ANU, Canberra 1975; D.K.G., Vol. 5, 27-30, D.K.Bl., 1900, 270-281.
2 The wording of this clause in D.K.G., Vol. 5, 30 differs, according to Peter and Bridget Sack, from that in D.K.Bl., 1900, 280 – the former source claiming that the wording in the latter was erroneous. The confusion arises because the German Parliament amended the text of this clause after the contract had been signed. D.K.G., vol. 5, 30 reproduces the original text as signed on 7th October 1898. D.K.Bl, 1900, 280, incorporates the subsequent amendment, however, it does indeed contain a minor error. Originally the Neu Guinea Kompagnie had been entitled to select the 50,000 hectares of land granted to it within ten

years, in New Britain (outside the Gazelle Peninsula) as well as Kaiser Wilhelmsland. Parliament reduced the time limit to three years and restricted the geographical area to Kaiser Wilhelmsland. D.K.Bl., 1900, 280, overlooked that in consequence of this amendment minor changes were required in subsequent, subordinate conditions and continues to speak of the "two main islands" – as opposed to the smaller off-shore islands – although the amendment had moved New Britain outside the scope of the contract. The text translated here is that reproduced in D.K.Bl., 1900, 280.

3 See note 2 above.
4 According to Peter and Bridget Sack, the German original uses the term "Grundbuchordnung" in an almost colloquial sense. The official title was *Imperial Order of the Chancellor of the Reich for the Imperial Ordinance of 20th July 1887 Regarding the Acquisition of Ownership and the Charging of Land in the Protectorate of the Neu Guinea Kompagnie,* of 30th July 1887.

Appendix 4

On the maintenance of international peace and security

Excerpt from statement by *Peter Donigi* on the report of the Special Committee on the Charter of the United Nations on the strengthening of the role of the organisation in particular on the draft declaration on fact-finding missions in the field of maintenance of international peace and security, delivered at the Sixth Committee Meeting on 4 October 1991

The UN fact-finding mission has to be mounted in a timely manner. Experience has proven that if any cause of dissension is not properly identified at the outset and dealt with, it is likely to fester just like a tropical ulcer or cancer until it is too late to use reason, mediation and consensus.

It is true to say that our very presence here and our participation alone is testimony to our concern about the maintenance of international peace and security within the territorial limits of our respective countries, the region and the world at large. Previous speakers have stated that fact-finding missions should diffuse rather then aggravate a dispute. However, fact-finding missions by their very expression, will not diffuse or aggravate a dispute or situation. The missions will only have the effect of delaying the adoption of irretractable positions by the parties to the dispute. This assumes that the missions will be mounted in a timely manner. They should create hope. They should create time within which some solutions can be found to the dispute.

It is through the collection and collation of true facts surrounding the causes of the dispute which will promote the work and functions of the United Nations and its organs as the catalyst for peace and security.

Accordingly, in considering the issue of consent of the receiving state, one must bear in mind the real purpose of the fact-finding mission. The real question is when a fact-finding mission seeks a state's consent to enter its territory, does it amount to intervention? If we limit the definition of "intervention" to a constructive and positive act to effect change in one's territory, then mere collection of information should not be interpreted as intervention. Collection of information forms the basis for determining the agenda items for conciliation and other peace facilitating process to take place.

The Declaration on Fact-Finding Missions should be viewed not as a document which validates intervention but as a document which facilitates the collection of true facts surrounding a particular dispute. Viewed in that perspective, should we then try to create barriers against fact-finding missions by demanding as a pre-condition the consent of the receiving state?

The sanctity of the territorial integrity of a state must be preserved. Yet on the other hand disputes between peoples within the state concerned have had the tendency of involving third parties, adjoining states and peoples of adjoining states.

If the dispute concerns the recognised democratic rights of "peoples" within states as recognised by the Charter, the Universal Declaration of Human Rights, the International Covenant on Economic, Social and Cultural Rights, the International Covenant on Civil and Political Rights etc., the burning question is, under those circumstances shouldn't the Member States agree to allow the fact-finding missions excess to their territory only in certain specified situations?

Some states are not parties or signatories to certain United Nations Conventions, Declarations or Resolutions concerning the democratic rights of "peoples". At least for states who are signatories, it should be possible for them to say, "yes, we have undertaken to provide to our citizens and peoples those rights, and an independent report of a visiting UN Mission will only insist in our government improving its relations and to provide better services to our peoples". What we must be seeking to do is to highlight and to emphasise the rule of law within certain agreed parameters. The United Nations Conventions, Declarations and Resolutions will have no meaning if there is no way of monitoring the extent of their recognition and application.

The indigenous peoples' rights to property and wealth from their land must be recognised and given effect to by the constitutional framework of a state.

The relationship between the Security Council and the General Assembly is that the Security Council can only act on matters referred to it by any organs of the United Nations or by a state. The wording of the Draft Declaration on Fact-Finding Missions should give definite instructions rather then to give the Security Council a discretion as to whether or not to conduct, undertake or commission a fact-finding mission. The United Nations Charter and the Declarations and Covenants on various rights talks about the rights of the "peoples". If we are to live by the language of the United Nations, then we must not provide for any discretion.

The request for a fact-finding mission should not be limited to states. The request mechanism should be extended to representative or representatives of a distinct people or peoples as at times it is the question of the rights of the peoples as against the encroachment by the state which has been the cause of dissension.

Appendix 5

On measures to prevent terrorism

Excerpt from statement by *Peter Donigi* to the Sixth Committee of the United Nations General Assembly on the report of the Secretary General on measures to prevent terrorism, delivered on 11 October 1991

Terrorism of any kind is abominable.

The Draft Resolution uses words that are very general giving the impression that they include all forms of terrorism but yet one is left with the feeling that the Resolution only deals with the violent forms of terrorism and not the other forms.

In order for us to appreciate the words "all acts, methods and practices of international terrorism" as is used in the Draft Resolution, we must think laterally and not be brow-beaten into dealing with only the violent forms of terrorism as the substantive paragraphs appear to portray.

Perhaps it is in the study of the causes of terrorism that one may appreciate that terrorism is not only in the violent act but could also be in the peaceful act disguised under what appears to be legitimate laws of the state concerned but yet amounts to a denial of the fundamental rights of the peoples concerned. The struggle for self-determination and national liberation quite often is associated with the struggle to preserve the right to language, culture, homeland, property, resources and wealth of the people. The laws of a state which deprives a person or group of people those legitimate rights, has no foundation either at natural law or at international law.

Accordingly, in defining "terrorism", should we limit it to violent acts or should we also be concerned with actions generally that are capable of creating anxiety or to coerce or induce a positive or negative response by threat. What then is the dictionary meaning? To terrorise is to fill with terror or anxiety or coerce by threat or violence. A conference to determine the extent and causes of terrorism is therefore justifiable.

The rights of the peoples should not be limited to peoples under colonial and racist regimes and other forms of alien domination and foreign occupation, to justify self-determination and independence. The rights of the indigenous peoples are also fundamental rights and which must be recognised and protected by the state within which is found those indigenous peoples or populations. In these situations, it is not the issue of self-determination and independence that is at stake. Quite the opposite. It is the preservation of a people and their right to property and wealth.

Colonialism was borne out of a desire to amass property and wealth. Thus the acquisition of property either by conquest, occupation, discovery or cession. The United Nations Charter, the various Resolutions, Declarations and Conventions on the rights of the "peoples" will have no meaning, if the United Nations and its organs do not play a part in protecting those rights, especially of peoples who desire only to have their rights acknowledged in a peaceful way. If these rights are not recognised, protected and enforced in a domestic situation, then should not the states concerned be classed and aligned as neo-colonists and be included in the agenda of the Fourth Committee?

In the Pacific, we have coconut crabs which have long retractable pincers inside their claws. They use those pincers to make a hole in the eye of the coconut and eat the flesh without cracking the coconut shell. If we do not protect the rights of these people, then ultimately when they finally, tired of abuse, demand (possibly by use of force) and get their right to self-determination, independence will be like the empty coconut shell. They will remain thirsty. They will remain hungry. The process has created a dependent child – the dependency syndrome.

The Declaration on Fact-Finding by the Organs of the United Nations will have no meaning if the causes (and history has always pointed to a denial of the natural rights of a group of people as the root cause) cannot be identified at an earlier stage before the situation deteriorates into violence. What better way to prevent violence then by recognising the rights of these indigenous peoples within a given state.

In Papua New Guinea, 97 percent of the landmass is owned by the indigenous peoples and title is determined according to the customary laws applicable in that particular area. It is common knowledge and universally accepted that title to land remains with each clan. Land is defined by custom as including the surface soil and what is above and below the surface to the centre of the earth. If this law is recognised and applied then all resources including minerals, petroleum, timber etc. become the property of the customary landowners and not the state.

Prior to Independence, the Australian mining and petroleum laws were applied to the country. Their laws say that all minerals and petroleum is the property of the state. On independence our Constitution recognised the right to property subject however to the right of the state to acquire property for a "public purpose". It is now questionable as to whether these mining and petroleum laws are indeed constitutional.

The mining and petroleum companies, mostly foreign multinationals, have established quite legitimately the Chamber of Mines and Petroleum to pursue, promote and protect their interests. They have now become so influential that, when some of my colleagues began questioning the desirability of vesting ownership of a pipeline between the oil fields in the highlands of Papua New Guinea to the offshore loading platform, some 250 kilometres away, in the consortium led by Chevron Corporation of United States, the Chamber and the consortium issued a threat to the people and the government of Papua New Guinea, which was headlined in our daily paper, to withdraw all their investments from the country.

The Chamber of Mines and Petroleum has also publicly voiced its opposition to the recognition of the fundamental rights of the landowners to their resources. They have indeed demanded of the state to maintain the status quo or face withdrawal *en masse* of the mining and petroleum companies from the country.

If "terrorism" is to fill with terror or anxiety or to coerce by threat but not violence, then would you say without doubt that Chevron Corporation, its consortium partners and the Chamber of Mines and Petroleum, are not practicing terrorism of the worst kind in Papua New Guinea?

In this day and age we should not adopt rules which will perpetuate the exploitation of the resources of the people, whose rights we have agreed to uphold and protect as fundamental. We should adopt rules which will assist them to exploit these resources – their resources. The distinguished jurist and former Commonwealth Secretary-General Sir Shridath Ramphal expressed the concern for the global need for a new world economic order more aptly when he said:

"Upholders of the System take it for granted that some countries are rich and others are poor and assume that by helping the rich to become more rich we will help the poor to become less poor. They ignore the possibility that some countries may be rich because others are poor and that the price of sustained growth in the developed world may be sustained poverty in the developing."[1]

Sir Shridath's comment is valid not only internationally but also domestically in certain countries where indigenous populations are found. Those who wield political, legislative and economic power within a state may ignore the possibility that they are rich because the indigenous populations, whose rights we have agreed to protect under the Charter and the various Resolutions and Covenants, are poor and that the price of sustained growth in that state may be sustained poverty of the indigenous peoples.

I have tried to show that the phrases "alien domination" and "foreign occupation" as are used in the Resolution (44/29) need not take the form of physical presence on one's territory. The super-imposition of foreign laws and ideologies which denies the fundamental rights of the indigenous peoples is as much an alien domination of the indigenous peoples as the physical presence of foreigners or aliens.

In the same way, the adoption and application of certain preconditions to provision of loan funds to "assist" in the development of local industry is as much an alien domination as the physical presence in one's territory. The creation of the dependency syndrome or continued dependency on alien or foreign assistance or suppliers of goods and services is as much an alien domination as the physical presence in one's territory.

Sir Shridath Ramphal once warned against the use of code words to shield indefensible status quo and said the word "confrontation" should not be used to an deny activist pursuit of consensus for change.[2] I hope what I have said is not seen as having the ability to create confrontation but should be seen as a positive identification of possible causes of confrontation which if not removed within a reasonable time could lead to parties adopting terrorist methods in an attempt to achieve their goals.

Notes appendix 5

1 Speech at Canada's 44th Couchiching Conference in 1975, reproduced in Barbara Ward's Selected Speeches of Shridath Ramphal, *One World to Share*, p. 11.
2 Speech on the theme of global inter-dependence to mark the diamond jubilee

of the English Speaking Union in London 11 July 1978, reproduced in Barbara Ward's Selected Speeches of Shridath Ramphal *One World to Share*, p. 128.

Appendix 6

On the code of crimes against peace and security

Excerpt from statement by *Peter Donigi* to the Sixth Committee of the United Nations General Assembly on the report of the international law commission on the draft articles on the code of crimes against peace and security of mankind, delivered on 6 November 1991

The United Nations Charter is akin to a constitution of a state. It provides for the institutions within which decisions can be made or taken in the interests of humanity. It lacks however, to a certain degree, the authority of a sovereign state. Its power and the extent of its authority is dependent on recognition of that authority or power by the sovereign state.

Nevertheless, the United Nations Charter is the basis, the foundation of "peoples' rights and freedoms". It is peoples' rights that moved the Security Council to act in the Gulf crisis. In this statement, I will concentrate on one of these fundamental rights – the right to property.

This right to property is further endorsed in the Universal Declaration of Human Rights adopted by the General Assembly in 1948, article 17 of which states:

> "1 Everyone has the right to own property alone as well as in association with others.
> "2 No one shall be arbitrarily deprived of his property."

In 1966, the General Assembly by Resolution 2200 adopted the International Covenant on Economic, Social and Cultural Rights and the International Covenant on Civil and Political Rights. Article 1 of both Covenants are identical and read as follows:

"1   All peoples have the right to self-determination. By virtue of that right they freely determine their political status and freely pursue their economic, social and cultural development.

"2   All peoples may, for their own ends, freely dispose of their natural wealth and resources without prejudice to any obligations arising out of international economic co-operation, based upon the principle of mutual benefit and international law. In no case may a people be deprived of its own means of subsistence."

Does the phrase "means of subsistence" relate to the phrase "natural wealth and resources" in the first sentence of the second paragraph? If such is the case, then it is conclusive that the rights of indigenous peoples all over the world at international law include their right to natural wealth and resources – however defined or described – on, in or under the surface of their land.

If the phrase "means of subsistence" is limited to rights pertaining to the use of the surface land, then is it not based on a desire and greed of governments or non-indigenous peoples to deprive the indigenous peoples of what is rightfully, by natural law, belongs to them?

For those countries with English common law systems, why is it that at common law, the customary law or *lex situ* supersedes the English common law in Wales and Scotland but in the other dominions and territories, the *lex situ* of the indigenous peoples are superseded by man-made laws based on a fictitious right of the sovereign to natural wealth and resources? Why is it that all of a sudden, the definition of land is limited to the surface soil and what is on top of it but does not include everything to the centre of the earth, when indeed that is the common law of England with the exception of gold and silver? Why is it that we must place a restriction on the definition of the term "property" so that it does not include mineral and petroleum resources below the surface of the earth when it is clear that the only distinction at common law is whether it is a "tangible" or an "intangible" property?

If the international community can accede the right of coastal states in respect to resources found in their continental shelf or economic zone, the why can't the international community recognise the indigenous peoples' right to sub-surface resources under their land? Resolution 41/132 of 4 december 1986 and Resolutions 43/123 and 43/124 of 1988 deal with the right to own property. The first preambular paragraph of Resolution 43/123 says:

> "*calling* its resolution 41/132 of 4 December 1986, in which it expressed the conviction that the full enjoyment by everyone of the right to own property alone as well as in association with others, as set forth in Article 17 of the Universal Declaration of Human Rights is of particular significance in fostering widespread enjoyment of other basic human rights and contributes to securing the goals of economic and social development enshrined in the Charter of the United Nations."

The substantive paragraph 4 of that Resolution urges states to provide:

> "… where they have not done so, adequate constitutional and legal provisions to protect the right of everyone to own property alone as well as in association with others and the right not to be arbitrarily deprived of one's property."

If we begin with the premise that indigenous peoples have always owned land and therefore the sub-surface resources *before* the introduction of constitutional and legal changes which differentiated between surface land and sub-surface resources, then that constitutional or legal change amounts to an arbitrary deprivation of their rights to sub-surface resources.

Substantive paragraph 3 of Resolution 43/124 of 1988 recognises that there exists in Member States many forms of legal property ownership "including private, communal and state forms, each of which should contribute to ensuring the effective development …"

Paragraph 4 of that Resolution on the other hand, calls upon states:

> "… to ensure that their national legislation with regard to all forms of property shall preclude any impairment of the enjoyment of human rights and fundamental freedoms …"

How can we justify that on the one hand we recognise their right to property and privacy on their land and on the other we take that right away by granting to third parties who have the wealth and technology, a better right to interfere with that right to property and privacy.

It appears we live in a world of contradictions. We adopt these Resolutions only to violate them within our own territories and we justify our actions by hiding behind the cloak of the sovereign right of state, the principles of non-aggression and non-intervention in the domestic affairs of another state and the territorial integrity of a state. At the same time we recognise the right of all "peoples" to self-determination and to freely pursue their economic, social and cultural development.

There is no explicit or specific mention of indigenous peoples in any United Nations instruments. However in all essential instruments the term "peoples" has been used. It is clear that the term "peoples" is not interchangeable with the term "state". Accordingly, state rights are distinguishable from peoples' rights.

The people in question must be capable of showing some common link, usually of an ethnic or historical kind, and must itself be capable of identifying its members. It could therefore include ethnic groups, tribes, linguistic groups and racial groups. The common link could also be the common ownership of land, as in all indigenous societies.

It would also seem that the right to self-determination is also applicable to "peoples" within the territory of Member States, if we are to give due recognition to that right. It is possible that these "peoples" may not want to exercise that right to self-determination but would prefer that their right to land and resources that the land entails be protected and enforced at the domestic level. They may want their right to "freely pursue their economic, social and cultural development" to be protected and given effect to at the domestic level by the governments of Member States.

The right to self-determination need not necessarily lead to secession or independence. It is conceivable that the right of self-determination does involve a right to determine the group's own socio-political and socio-economic framework within a state. In that perspective, the state must recognise the indigenous peoples' rights as outlined in the various United Nations instruments and must create the necessary constitutional and legal framework for enforcing those rights. Those who continue to deny or refuse to acknowledge the rights of the indigenous peoples are not pursuing an expansionist aim – that has already been achieved in the creation of the state – but are pursuing nothing less than an exploitationist objective driven on by mere human greed; the desire to accumulate wealth at the expense of the native populations or landowners.

The Commission on Human Rights through the Sub-Commission on Prevention of Discrimination and Protection of Minorities has for some time been considering a draft Universal Declaration on Indigenous Rights. The draft Declaration sets out in what appears to be exhaustive form, the rights of the indigenous peoples. Part III of that draft specifically deals with land rights and mineral and other sub-surface resources. It specifically distinguishes between surface rights and other sub-surface rights. Yet paragraph 1 of Part 1 of the draft guarantees them the right:

> "... to full and effective enjoyment of all fundamental rights and freedoms ... which are universally recognised in the Charter of the United Nations and in existing international human rights instruments."

Paragraph 2 thereof guarantees them:

> "... the right to be free and equal to all other human beings in dignity and rights and to be free from adverse distinction or discrimination of any kind."

In one document alone we have found this contradiction. There is no doubt that the indigenous peoples' right to property is a fundamental right at international law. By distinguishing surface rights from sub-surface rights, we have not only discriminated against these "peoples" but more importantly taken away their right to future wealth, resources and their "own means of subsistence". We have by this draft Declaration on Indigenous Rights qualified or restricted the meaning of the terms "peoples" and "property" as used in the instruments quoted earlier. What this draft does is to say that the term "peoples" as used in the Charter and the Covenants does not include indigenous peoples and in so far as it includes them it only refers to certain rights and not all fundamental rights. What this draft does is to say that the term "property" as used in the Charter and the Covenants includes all property except sub-surface elements under land owned by indigenous peoples. This draft, if adopted, is discrimination at its worst, by the very body that is supposed to protect the rights of indigenous peoples.

The draft Code on Crimes deals with all situations involving aggression, intervention, colonial and other forms of alien domination, genocide, apartheid, systematic or mass violations of human rights, mercenaries, international terrorism, etc. Nowhere in this draft code can be found crimes against the rights of indigenous peoples, especially their rights to property and sub-surface resources.

The denial of the right to property must be included as a crime against those peoples' humanity.

When there was a call for deep sea resources to be made the common heritage of mankind, coastal states demand exclusivity and developed the concepts of economic zones, archipelagic states, and continental shelf to define what is within the jurisdiction of coastal states and what is not. If we apply the same reasoning, then should not the rights of the indigenous peoples to sub-surface resources under their defined territory take precedence over state rights?

The draft Article 15 on aggression is plain. It deals with the use of force by one state against another state. Yet on the other hand the words: "... or in any other manner inconsistent with the Charter of the United Nations" would lead us to believe that it is possible that the state using the armed force not against another state but in any other manner inconsistent with the Charter is capable of being guilty of aggression and therefore within the meaning of that crime.

If such is the case then would it not be possible for a state to commit the crime of aggression if it uses its armed forces (be it military or civilian) to deny the indigenous peoples rights to sub-surface resources or to prohibit them from exercising ownership rights to those resources?

I noted that paragraph 7 of Article 15 of the draft Code deals with the right of peoples under "colonial and racist regimes or other forms of alien domination" to self-determination, freedom and independence. It envisages that to qualify for the right to be heard by the United Nations, the indigenous peoples must first of all seek self-determination, freedom and independence before they can be granted *locus standi* to come before us. I put it to you that by the time they get to that stage, violence would have taken place. Do we only have to resolve after the event – after the spilling of blood?

We talk about peaceful means of solving disputes between states, yet we have not settled on a constructive mechanism for settling disputes between states and their indigenous peoples. Should we continue to allow these disputes to be resolved before their domestic courts when we know that in some instances the domestic laws on the subject are contrary to recognised fundamental rights? Under what circumstances and before which courts can these indigenous peoples bring their complaint and demand that their rights be respected and more importantly, protected?

The effect of these Resolutions and draft Codes is to give further impetus to indigenous peoples all over the world to demand their right to self-determination – in the secessionist sense. Because it is only through that process that they can be heard. We should be working towards fomenting and cementing the relationships between indigenous peoples and their neighbours within states – not providing an avenue for them to break away and to create hundreds of other smaller states.

I am also concerned that systematic violation of human rights may take place over a longer period of time such that if one views one incident in isolation one may come to the conclusion that it is not or does not amount to systematic violation of human rights. States or agents of states could very well carry on their activities in such a manner in complete disregard for those rights and yet avoid being caught by this draft Code.

A crime is a crime however organised and perpetrated. A single violation is no less a violation than a systematic or mass violation.

Why then can we not adopt an approach which identifies situations where state sovereignty cannot be invoked or claimed to legitimise the abuse of the internationally recognised rights and freedoms either of the individual or a recognised group of people?

Appendix 7

An Introduction to the International Covenants on Human Rights

Excerpt from the Commonwealth Secretariat publication, "An Introduction to the International Covenants on Human Rights"[1] by *Paul Sieghart*

Human rights and development

Everyone today – and not least the members of the Commonwealth – is only too painfully aware of the glaring differentials between the states of economic development of different countries – that is, the painful differences between what are sometimes (though not always accurately as a matter of geography) called the rich "North" and the poor "South". Whatever the terminology, there can be no doubt that, for all but the richest nations, economic development must be a paramount objective for any responsible government.

On this subject, there is no shortage of international resolutions and declarations – including the Commonwealth's own New Delhi Statement of 1983. But what is the situation in the international legal order?

Article 1 of the Covenants has already been cited, but it is worth citing its first paragraph again, this time with added emphasis:

> "All peoples have the right of self-determination. By virtue of that right they freely determine their political status and freely pursue their economic, social and cultural development."

Earlier drafts referred only to status, and not to development. But what is perhaps most striking about this phraseology is that it speaks not only of economic development – which is the concept of "development" most commonly at the forefront of governmental policies, and of their peoples' minds – but in the same breath of their "social and cultural" development. (It should be recalled here that the preamble to each of the Covenants specifically refers to the other, pointing out that "the ideal of free human beings enjoying freedom from fear and want can only be achieved if conditions are created whereby everyone may enjoy" the rights declared in both the Covenants).

This language provides a pointer to an important insight – namely that "development" is not a purely economic matter. True, so long as people suffer avoidably from starvation or malnutrition there will be a gross violation of their fundamental human rights – but so, likewise, will there be if they live, with full bellies and adequate housing, in a state in which they can only express their opinions at the peril of being persecuted, and perhaps incarcerated for years on end. Development, in short, is more that merely a matter of economic advance.

To cite the conclusions of an international conference of experts convened by the International Commission of Jurists in The Hague in 1981:

> "Development should ... be seen as a global concept including, with equal emphasis, civil and political rights and economic, social and cultural rights ...
>
> "True development requires a recognition that the different human rights are inseparable from each other, and development is inseparable from human rights and the Rule of Law. Likewise, justice and equity at the international level are inseparable from justice and equity at the national level ...
>
> "Development should be understood as a process designed progressively to create conditions in which every person can enjoy, exercise and utilise under the Rule of Law all his human rights, whether economic, social, cultural, civil or political.
>
> "Every person has the right to participate in, and benefit from, development in the sense of a progressive improvement in the standard and quality of life.
>
> "The concept of the right to development ... serves to express the right of all peoples all over the world, and of every citizen, to enjoy all human rights.
>
> "The primary obligation to promote development, in such a way as to satisfy this right, rests upon each state for its own territory and for the

persons under its jurisdiction. As the development process is a necessary condition for peace and friendship between nations, it is a matter of international concern, imposing responsibilities upon all states.

"Consequently, a state promoting its own development within its available resources is entitled to the support of other states in the implementation of its policies." [2]

Clear echoes of this language may be found in the recent Declaration on the Right of Development adopted by the UN General Assembly.[3] This proclaims the right to development as an inalienable human right, and declares in its Preamble

> "that development is a comprehensive economic, social,cultural and political process, which aims at the constant improvement of the well-being of the entire population and of all individuals on the basis of their active, free and meaningful participation in development and in the fair distribution of benefits resulting therefrom."

Omelettes and eggs

One of the more cynical propositions of politics is that "you cannot make omelettes without breaking eggs". As a homely proverb, the proposition has its attractions; what is less clear is whether, at all events in the field of economic development, there is any empirical evidence to support it – or whether it is a mere assertion of ideology. Is it really the case, as some governments defensively claim, that you cannot create the benefits of economic development for a nation without violating, at least temporarily, the human rights of a substantial number of its citizens? So far, what little research has been done on the subject has failed to establish this as an empirical proposition;[4] the evidence seems rather to indicate that respect for the individual human rights – civil, political, economic, social, and cultural – of a nation's inhabitants promotes, rather than hinders, that nation's economic development, not to mention its development on the social and cultural planes.

Whatever may be the correct view on this question, it is clear that the Covenants fully support the objective of "development" in all its forms. At the same time, they do not afford to the government of any state that adheres to them any pretext for abridging or denying the human rights of the inhabitants of its state, in the purported interests of economic development alone.

Notes appendix 7

1 Reproduced from "An Introduction to the International Covenents on Human Rights", a Paper prepared for the Commonwealth Secretariat by Paul Sieghart, 1988, pp. 12-14.
2 *Development, Human Rights and the Rule of Law* (Oxford 1981), pp. 225-6.
3 Resolution 41/128 of 4 December 1986.
4 See Sieghart, P., "Economic Development, Human Rights, and the Omelette Thesis", *Development Policy Review*, Vol. 1, No. 1 (London, May 1983).

Appendix 8

On Developmentism and Constitutionalism

Address by Peter Donigi to members of the Papua New Guinea Australia business council held in Port Moresby on 11 October 1990

> *"Since, then, we know what it is to fear the Lord, we try to persuade men. What we are is plain to God, and I hope it is also plain to your conscience.*
> *"We are not trying to commend ourselves to you but are giving you an opportunity to take pride in us, so that you can answer those who take pride in what is seen rather than what is in the heart.*
> *"If we are out of our mind, it is for the sake of God; if we are in our right mind, it is for you."*
>
> 2 Corinthians 5:11-13

This country is a Christian country. The Constitution said so. When the Constitution was adopted, the Constituent Assembly said:

> "We, the people of Papua New Guinea pledge ourselves to guard and pass on to those who come after us our noble traditions and the Christian principles that are now ours."

All the Christian principles are reproduced in one form or another in the Constitution. You need only to read the national Goals and Directive Principles, the Basic Rights and the Basic Social Obligations to understand what I mean. I have therefore begun this address by quoting from Saint Paul's second letter to the Corinthians. Saint Paul was writing at a time when his enemies were asserting that he was suffering from religious mania, pointing perhaps to the sensational conversion he claimed to have experienced on the road to Damascus and to what they regarded as his insane way of life. He does not deny the assertion by his enemies that he was out of his mind. The whole letter shows how willingly and joyfully he endured affliction for the truth (Gospel). He says if those who take pride in what is seen (material things), consider him to be out of his mind, then that is a matter essentially between him and God to whom he is accountable. What is important is what is in the heart.

Over the last few years I have been vocal about the issues of ownership of resources. This year I was vocal on greater and effective participation by Papua New Guineans, especially landowners. I do not wish to reiterate those concerns here. I merely wish to say that I have not changed my mind. I stand by what I have written, even if it means having to be branded a racist (as some contributors to the *Post Courier* newspaper have alleged). As a matter of principle, I do not and will not enter into written dialogue or correspondence with those who use *nom de plumes*, and unlike Saint Paul, I hold such people in utter and absolute contempt.

During my speech at the opening of the Legal Conference in August to commemorate the Chief Justice's 10 years in office, I said:

> "There is no need for us to go looking under the stones in far away countries to determine the appropriate laws for adoption in Papua New Guinea. After all what is a rule of law ... to be applied in a given circumstance or set of circumstances? ... Section 9 of the Constitution is exhaustive as to the applicable laws ... The grey areas appear to be around the underlying laws and what is meant by a customary rule of law ... The time is ripe for change in our laws in order to properly reflect the desires and aspirations and the traditional norms and values of Papua New Guineans ... We have to start somewhere."

During the conference, however, I was most impressed with papers delivered by Graham Powell and Anthony Reagan of the University of Papua New Guinea and John Millett of the Institute of National Affairs. Mr Powell's paper made the following points:

a   The underlying laws of Papua New Guinea can not be developed because the average citizens cannot obtain the services of private lawyers to assert, protect and promote their interests.

b   The primary role of developing the underlying law of Papua New Guinea is given to the Supreme and National Courts and an Act of Parliament can only be declaratory after a significant body of law has been developed and tested through time by the Courts.

c   The Section 19 References directly to the Supreme Court as a means of developing the underlying law has been disappointing. In this regard Mr Powell said:

> "Since Independence in 1975 the Supreme Court has only been given the opportunity to venture a worthwhile opinion as to the validity of its young Constitution and diverse constitutional and other laws on thirteen occasions. This is less than one each year."

d   He concluded that:

> "Whereas the preoccupation in other jurisdictions quite properly centres around court efficiency, and maybe even discouraging litigation by alternative means of dispute resolution, the preoccupation in Papua New Guinea in the next ten years should be quite the opposite. As many litigants as possible should be encouraged and enabled to take actions to the Courts, which, it must be hoped, will continue to provide a rule of law with the efficiency and ability that they have demonstrated in the last ten years."

Anthony Regan's paper on the other hand focused on the extent to which the goal of the law becoming a legitimising ideology for the new state has been achieved and the contribution of the Courts towards the achievement of that goal. In it, he argued that economic and political factors are significant obstacles in the limited impact of constitutionalism in Papua New Guinea.

What is Constitutionalism?
Constitutionalism is the operation of effective restraints.

What is a Rule of Law?
There is no such thing as a rule of law unless the following factors exist in a given society:
a   the territory of a state,
b   a recognised authority to issue and enforce commands, and
c   the mass or subjects who willingly recognise the authority as capable of issuing and enforcing those commands.

Max Weber argues that in any political order, three main types of legitimate authority can be found and in all cases the three may co-exist at any given time. He identified them as traditional, charismatic and legal-rational. The legal rational type is peculiar to Western European States. It is the rule of law which justifies and legitimises the economic and political order of the capitalist states. Regan in his paper quoted Professor Ghai as saying that the rule of law continues to be important to these states because the rule of law has

> "... become part of the political and cultural tradition of the Western State, deeply rooted in its organic growth ... It appeals because of its resonance with modernity of the western sciences and society."

Regan further acknowledged Ghai as saying that, in third world countries, the lack of that social cohesion makes legitimacy of the rule of law a central question. The rule of law is attractive because it could possibly transcend these social conditions but, without the inherent economic, political and cultural pre-conditions, it will be difficult to maintain. In these countries, there are neither the historical conditions nor the commitment to the rule of law from those in authority that will tend to flow from their desire to claim legitimacy through law. Professor Ghai says:

> "If the rule of law as an ideology is unimportant, it will come as no surprise that it is also unimportant in its substantive aspect."

In respect to constitutionalism, Ghai was quoted by Regan as saying that in developing countries

> "some of the competing ideologies invoked as legitimation are clearly inimical to constitutionalism. Ghai nominates developmentalism; the charismatic legitimacy of extremely personalised power of presidential rule in many African and Asian countries; religion; and racism. To these might be added the closely related phenomenon of the creation by those in authority of a 'siege mentality' in response to external threat or crisis of internal subversion. What must be emphasised here is that by resort to these competing ideologies not only do the rulers seek to justify their rule, but they also seek to justify increasingly strong central power, reduced democracy and reduced emphasis on the rights of the individual. Needless to say, they also

normally involve attempts to entrench the power of a narrow interest group."

Regan continued:

"Brief analysis of these competing ideologies is required ... public debates in Papua New Guinea suggest that only religion does not have the potential to become a serious contender for legitimising a state where formal legal restraints on the exercise of governmental powers are much reduced. In relation to the first two factors, the justification in Africa and elsewhere for strengthened state structures, curtailing of political activity and reduced emphasis on individual's rights is often the need for economic development or for 'nation building'. Developmentalism is in turn closely linked with the supremacy of a single political party and the deification of its leader. Racism is often used as a unifying and legitimising device, as with expulsion of or restrictions on Asians in East Africa and the promotion of Malay and Fijian interests in Malaysia and Fiji respectively. A siege mentality is often encouraged by fear of the outside threats, as in the case of Singapore, but equally often by exploitation of racist fears, as in Malaysia and Fiji."

Mr Regan then reviewed the constitution-making process and the conflict between the desires of the Constitutional Planning Committee and the government and concluded as follows:

"There are a range of factors which arguably impact the development of constitutionalism in Papua New Guinea. While it is not possible to analyse them fully, they require brief comment as they provide some insights into the causes of what may yet prove to be a crisis for the constitutionalism in Papua New Guinea. They include several closely related factors:
- the role of the state;
- the relative weakness of the executive government and consequential weakness and relative autonomy of important institutions (including those responsible for the use of coercion, namely the Police and the Defence Forces);
- the relative weakness of the impact of formal law; and

- the influence (arguably growing) of competing ideologies."

In relation to the first issue Regan quoted Ghai as saying:

"... As the state is the primary instrument of accumulation, corruption is no mere pathology, but becomes endemic, woven into the very fabric of the apparatus of the state. The pressure towards corruption arises not only from the economic greed but also the imperativeness of political survival, since the primary basis of a politicians support is, generally, not party or other political platform, but clientilism (which is sustained by regular favours to one's followers). Public control and accountability over the apparatus cannot therefore be permitted. On the other hand, resistance on the part of the exploited is met principally by coercion, and the state becomes authoritarian as well as irresponsible (in the sense of public accountablity) ... Is this true of Papua New Guinea today? There is growing evidence of corruption and failure to deal with that phenomenon."

In relation to the second issue, Regan says that

"The capacity of the executive government has not increased since independence, and the ability of the central decision-making authority to direct and control activities is arguably weaker than in the colonial period due largely to political instability, itself a factor of the weak party system and constant shifting of political alliances. In these circumstances, major elements of the government apparatus, relatively weak in capacity, are left with very great autonomy. The results contribute to the relatively limited impact of the formal law – the 1984 Clifford Report estimated that 80 percent of crime was never dealt with by police – development of patterns of illegal or extra legal activities by governmental bodies.
"As regards the impact of formal law, there is constant evidence that the law is often of little concern to those whose primary responsibility is its enforcement. The abuses of human rights in North Solomons and the law and order operations in the highlands provide examples. The result can be contempt for the law in the minds of those affected, who may well regard it as an instrument of repression."

> "As to competing ideologies there is already evidence that 'developmentalism' has the potential to justify moves for increased central government controls and reduced emphasis on individual rights. In the same context, there is evidence of a siege mentality developing in relation to law and order and related problems which is likely to be used to justify the same directions.
>
> "The factors just outlined may suggest the likelihood of fairly grim prospects for constitutionalism. But it must be admitted that the Papua New Guinea political system has demonstrated great resilience in part because of the spread of power among institutions, offices and level of government – the wisdom of the Constitutional Planning Committee in this regard has been vindicated."

John Millet

John Millet on the other hand gave us a lecture on John Raul's theories of justice and concluded:

> "The interdependence between economics and justice, in both its general meaning and its narrower one of law and order, manifests most forcefully in the grossly inadequate labour absorption in Papua New Guinea today. If we do not get the economics of this problem right we will continue in the 1990s as we have done in the 1980s to place increasing demand on the law and order agencies – on the police, on the courts and the corrective institutions – and to move inexorably away from, rather than towards, a just society – away from not towards integral human development."

Consciously or unconsciously Millet, the only non-lawyer who delivered a paper at the conference, like Powell and Regan brought forth the issue of constitutionalism and the rule of law for "interdependence" and "integral human development" as "developmental" issues, if one were to apply Professor Ghai's assertions.

The issue at stake for the investors is not what this government can do to get out of the eye of the "wiliwili" (cyclone). In my view no amount of rhetoric or white papers can get it out of that "wiliwili". It is with the help of foreign investors, "moving inexorably away from", to borrow from Millet, constitutionalism. For constitutionalism to prevail there must be a redirection of attitudes, philosophies and a conscious effort by all institutions of government and capital (domestic and foreign) towards Papua New Guinean forms of participation, consultation and consensus and a continuous renewal of the responsiveness of these institutions to the needs and attitudes of the people of Papua New Guinea. This requirement is already specified in the first directive principle of the fifth national goal in the Constitution.

In recognising that developmentalism has the potential to justify moves for increased central government controls and reduced emphasis on individual rights, we all must work together to get out of that "wiliwili" by adopting a positive approach to constitutionalism.

Secondly, John Millet is of the view that integral human development cannot be achieved without government review of its policies. I too hold that view, but mine is based on constitutionalism. I understand his is based on state ownership of all resources from which all good things are to be redistributed in the form of goods and services. Without be-labouring the issue, Ghai makes the point that the circumstances in which a state arose in Africa, not organically out of civil society and not reflecting economic realities, makes a state a central force in the process of accumulation and reproduction. This in turn leads to corruption and repression. My point is whilst it is true that PNG was not organically born out of a civil society and that its birth does not reflect underlying economic realities, the process of accumulation and reproduction is not conceived in the Constitution as solely a function of the state. As such, the process of accumulation, reproduction and redistribution should only be achieved by adoption of taxation and other fiscal measures, rather than through direct involvement and ownership of businesses and property rights.

On 1st October 1990, I watched a progamme on ABC television about avoidance of tax in Australia and the tax office's investigation into the affairs of the top 100 companies. Towards the end of the programme, the issue of the effectiveness of the tax office in pursuing these tax avoiders was raised amidst knowledge of possible political contact and corporate lobby. The issue was whether the Tax Office should have withdrawn a tax directive without allowing it to go before the courts for interpretation.

In my view important issues concerning the validity of or interpretations of legislations or whether or not certain directives could be *ultra vires*, the powers of the issuing agency must not be decided by political compromises and "avoidance" of the proper functioning of the relevant institutions of government.

We in Papua New Guinea have witnessed and no doubt will continue to witness the power of corporate lobbying and "developmentalism". This lobby has taken the form of threats to the government and the people of this country. The threats are assumed and, when given recognition by the government, become an effective tool to support or forge the creation of the "siege mentality" by those in government. The threats take two forms – withdrawal of investment and an allegation to sue for damages.

In succumbing to the weight of economic pressures and foreign corporate interests, our politicians have effectively compromised constitutionalism for developmentalism. The latest veiled threat to use force in the Hides Gas project issued by the Acting Prime Minister, Mr Ted Diro, is evidence of such "siege mentality" at work (1st October issue of *Post Courier*, page 12). I am afraid once compromised there is no turning back unless there is a change of government or players in the field.

I wonder whether it has occurred to the government and the investors who rely on government by acquisition and government by force to legitimise their claims over the rights of customary landowners, that the customary landowners would also develop a "siege mentality" to justify their use of force, however crude, to defend their rights.

I pose the following questions for you to ponder and decide which team you would rather support – developmentalism or constitutionalism.

1. Do you believe in constitutionalism or the rule of law or would you prefer a dictatorial government without a constitution and a bill of rights?
2. If you prefer constitutionalism and the rule of law, why are you promoting political solutions to issues which have to be resolved by the third arm of government, namely the National Judicial System?
3. What can you as an Australian businessman do to help save this country from the impending perils?

My preference is to adopt, observe and implement constitutionalism or the rule of law and reject those who take pride in what is seen rather than what is in in the heart.

In the issue of exploitation of major resources, there is no way that the government can be judged guilty of misrepresenting the state of the laws in this country. Large muti-national corporations are used to investing or operating in very many different types of legal systems throughout the world. They therefore have built up the legal capacity to review the systems and the laws before making investment decisions. Consultancy lawyers make enough fees out of the whole exercise and do carry large professional indemnity insurance policies. The investors therefore do have recourse against lawyers who have failed to understand that our legal system is based on our autochthonous Constitution and not entirely on the English legal system.

I began by quoting the Bible. I shall end with it.

"If the blind lead the blind, both shall fall into the ditch."
Matthew 15:14.

Appendix 9

The Constitution and Human Rights[1]

The Papua New Guinea Constitution provided for the rights of the individual in almost all aspects of human relations. I say "almost" because it is becoming evident after 16 years of testing in the Courts of Papua New Guinea that it may not have covered all aspects of human relations.

The division in the Constitution which deals with human rights began with a declaration that a person can do anything he wishes to do so long as his act or omission does not interfere with the exercise of the rights of others. Questions have now been raised in our courts as to the effect of this section. Is it merely declaratory of the common law rules as they exist in England on 15th September 1975 (the schedule to the Constitution adopted the principles and rules of common law and equity as they existed in England on that date) or is it intended to give a constitutional validity to an act or omission of a person in the exercise of his rights under the Constitution and therefore enforceable as a constitutional law. In other words, is it a constitutional right in itself capable of enforcement.

The right to an impartial and fair trial and the freedom from inhuman treatment has on the other hand been fully tested and it appears now that the law is quite clear on the subjects of

a   prolonged incarceration in jails without trials,
b   harsh and oppressive treatment of prisoners,
c   the right to be given a fair hearing, and
d   the right to a judicial review even after the expiry of the statutory period for filing appeals.

Of interest is the provision which provides that all acts done under or pursuant to a valid law but is nevertheless harsh or oppressive or is disproportionate to the circumstances of the particular case is an unlawful act.

The Supreme Court had found that the provision is not a right or freedom capable of being enforced by a grieving party as any other constitutional right. It found the provision to be merely declaratory. An individual must therefore found his action under some other right under the Constitution as a last will and testament; it does not promote the philosophy of all constitutional lawyers that a Constitution must be a living document capable of interpretation and application to the changing circumstances the country may find itself in.

The provision which deals with right to official information and freedom to hold and publish information has yet to be tested. We have had situations where politicians have threatened to curtail or restrict the right to freedom of the press. They have however refrained from doing so because of the publicity given to the possible effects of such a law not only on the peoples' right to information but also the parliamentarians own right to information as well as their right to hold and publish their opinions. The right to official information has not been tested because by and large official government agencies have been forthcoming in responding to Summonses to Produce Evidence or to provide official records.

In the area of the power of the Minister for Foreign Affairs to issue deportation orders without specifying the reasons, it has been held that the Minister can do that subject to compliance with the rules of natural justice, the minimum requirement of which is the right to be heard. The rules of natural justice are also provided for in the Constitution but the courts have now held that the provision of the Constitution does not create a constitutional right but is merely declaratory of the common law rules. Another case of reading the Constitution like the last will and testament?

The right to freedom of employment, as far as I can recall, has never been tested in the Courts nor has the right to freedom of association or of belonging to an association. Questions which could be raised in respect to the exercise of this right would be the right to form or establish exclusive social clubs, membership of which would be restricted to one or the other of the sexes, the origins or racial background or the income level of the members.

This right, if read with the right to equality of all citizens, could well raise questions concerning the validity or otherwise of membership fees. If membership fees are set at a level higher than the *per capita* income of any citizen, should it be held as depriving the citizen of an equal opportunity to be a member of the social club?

The right to hold and to stand for public office has been well tested in the Courts. Every possible interpretation has been given to the relevant provisions, primarily because the country has experienced a high degree of the losing candidates filing electoral petitions to the Court of Disputed Returns. Of immense surprise to me personally, was the decision of the Supreme Court overturning the previous decision of another Supreme Court in 1983 which held that any law which sets the nomination fees at K 1,000 to be unconstitutional as denying the right of a citizen to stand for and to hold public office. In the 1983 case as Counsel for the Ombudsman Commission, I was able to show to the court that an average citizen earned less than K 300 per annum. I am confident that the per capita income of a citizen has not exceeded K 1,000 per annum and the recent law which was introduced by sitting Members of Parliament to set the nomination fees as K 1,000 was designed to reduce the number of candidates, thereby giving the sitting members an unfair advantage. The previous nomination fee was K 100.00.

It appeared that the reasoning of a recent Supreme Court decision was based on the fact that Papua New Guineans, by tradition, will be required to contribute to the cost of meeting the campaign costs of another clan member. This decision runs contrary to the Organic Law on leadership which requires that a leader, including a politician, not place himself in a situation where he could be seen to be compromised in the exercise of his official duties. A Member of Parliament who borrows from his clan to pay for his nomination fee and other costs will be forever indebted to the clan, resulting in possible unfair distribution of future benefits throughout his electorate.

The "first past the post" electoral system has created problems already where larger clans appear to get representation in Parliament at the expense of smaller clans. We do not require an additional incentive, such as the upholding of a law which is clearly unconstitutional, to perpetuate the existing imbalance in the distribution of benefits.

The right to unjust deprivation of property has not been fully tested in the courts. In one case involving a private citizen against a company, the Court appeared to favour the view that the right to unjust deprivation of property can only be enforced against the state and not against another private citizen. Another case also involving a private citizen but this time against the state challenging the validity of the Mining and Petroleum legislations as amounting to deprivation of a customary landowner's right to property in minerals and petroleum, was rejected on the grounds of *locus standi* and therefore the main issue had yet to be decided. An appeal has been filed and heard on the *locus standi* issue but as of today's date a decision is yet to be handed down by the Supreme Court.

Of interest now is the Mount Kare case, which has been bogged down with technicalities. In that case the landowners themselves have challenged the constitutional validity of the Mining Act which declared the property in the gold under their land as being state property. The question of *locus standi* will therefore not be an issue. This case is of interest to all mining and petroleum companies operating in Papua New Guinea.

I have managed to cover some rights that may be of interest to the participants. These are rights which are provided for in our Constitution. Some have been read down to be merely declaratory of common law. Such a reading demeans the provisions in our Constitution which called for the Courts of our country to develop the underlying law. I am sure that was not the intention of the Members of our Constituent Assembly which adopted our Constitution. It also demeans the statement that our Constitution is "truly autochthonous". It is not if we have to borrow from the English common law to interpret and apply its provisions.

A further question is whether or not the constitutional rights are enforceable against private citizens or corporations. Clearly some are possible and others are not, meaning they are only enforceable against the state. Where do we draw a line between common law rights and constitutional rights. It would appear to me that the rules in *Rylands v. Fletcher* and *Donohue v. Stephenson* appear to be well catered for in the provision dealing with the right to do anything that does not interfere with the rights of others (first mentioned above). Yet our Courts have found our constitutional provision to be merely declaratory. If so, then what purpose do such provisions serve – merely to make the Constitution look thick and feel heavy for some lawyers to wave around in the face of an unsuspecting public to display ostensible authority?

The right to development which has been debated in various United Nations bodies has yet to find itself into our legislations let alone Constitution. It was certainly debated well before 1975 but was not thought to be an essential human right to be included in the Constitution. My reading of the Constitutional Planning Report leaves me with the conclusion that it was never considered. Likewise, under the circumstances, should not one consider the rights to education, health services and drinkable water as basic rights which should have been included in a Constitution?

Papua New Guinea is a country where 97 percent of the land is owned collectively by clans and rights of ownership and use of the land are determined by the unwritten customary laws of the clan. Almost all of the land is unsurveyed and unregistered. Does the right to development involve an obligation on the part of the state to adopt policies which would facilitate rather than retard the use of customary land and the resources it entails for the profit and gain of the landowning clans and its members? Should such policies involve a review of the banking structures and policies to facilitate loans to be made to landowning clans for such purposes? If a bank was to refuse such a loan, should the landowning clans be given a constitutional right to challenge the decision of the bank based on the commercial viability of the project?

Is that a country that I would want to be part of? Should I be proud of my heritage as a member of a clan within a distinct linguistic group within Papua New Guinea? Should the political structure be redefined so as to protect and preserve my heritage? If it should be changed, then should I not be allowed to utilise my God-given heritage which includes rights to land and all the resources it entails, to develop or exploit those resources with the best technology there is in the world for the benefit of my clan and my people?

These are all relevant questions which are or should be asked by Papua New Guineans, exercising their constitutional right to hold and to publish those opinions without fear of any repercussions. It is only in the free exchange of opinions, that a country can be said to be truly democratic. Above all else the Constitution must guarantee that freedom of speech and it must be protected at all costs.

The right to property was debated in the United Nations in the 1950s and found its way into the Universal Declaration of Human Rights, the International Covenant on Economic, Social and Cultural Rights and the International Covenant on Civil and Political Rights. Papua New Guinea is not a homogeneous society. It is made up of many different peoples and linguistic groups. We have a Constitution which on its face recognises the rights of these different peoples and linguistic groups. Yet the policies of successive governments since Independence appear to be aimed at the destruction of the identity of our individual peoples. It is aimed at creating a nation of selfless individuals devoid of history prior to the so-called European discovery of their roots.

After 18 years, it is now clear in my own mind that the Constitution of Papua New Guinea needs amending in order to avoid the awful trend that our Courts have appeared to establish and which our Constitutional Planning Committee warned us about – the reading of its provisions as if it is the last will and testament.

Note appendix 9
1 Paper reproduced from the Commonwealth Institute publication "Human Rights: The Commonwealth and Europe" by Peter Donigi, Report of the Seminar, 4th June 1992, pp. 30-34.

Appendix 10

Briefing paper: Papua New Guinea Common Carrier Pipeline Company

1   Background
Immediate NEC (National Executive Council) decision is required to separate pipeline ownership from oil production.

The Kutubu Joint Venture oil production project is now imminent. We understand that Chevron, as Operator for the joint licence holders of PPL100, and the Department of Minerals and Energy are well advanced in the full spectrum of reviews and negotiations leading to the issue of a Petroleum Development Licence this year. We assume that the state is likely to exercise its option under the Petroleum Act to take a carried interest of up to 22.5 percent in the venture, with the associated "accumulated liability".

The project will require the construction and operation of a pipeline from the Southern Highlands to a moored export terminal in the Gulf of Papua. We expect that the capital cost of this essential infrastructure is likely to be in the range of K 300 – K 350 million, including capitalised interest during the construction. Current thinking is that it will be owned and funded by the Kutubu Joint Venture.

2   Beneficial features of a common carrier
No one oil producer should be sole owner of the pipeline. Common carrier status will improve commercial prospects of other oil fields in the Fold Belt.

The pipeline and export terminal required for the Kutubu Joint Venture are essential project infrastructure facilities, and are strategic national assets. There is every likelihood that these facilities will soon be called upon to transport oil from other discoveries in tenements in the Papuan Fold Belt.

We suggest that such infrastructure is too important to be owned and controlled by any one group of oil producers. Experience in other countries has shown that legislative provisions cannot be relied upon to enforce true common carrier status of producer-owned pipelines. Hence, we believe that petroleum exploration and development in Papua New Guinea would be well served by having ownership and control of strategic infrastructural facilities independent of producers. A common carrier company, providing an independent service, would make capacity available to all producers on an arm's length basis. Participants in other Petroleum Prospecting Licences in the vicinity of the pipeline would perceive enhanced economic prospectivity of their tenements, and be more willing to commit risk capital to exploration and development, with the knowledge that they would have access to the pipeline on open terms.

A successful independent pipeline company, owned to a significant extent by Papua New Guinean investors, could also stimulate the development of other private sector infrastructure businesses.

3 Monticello Enterprises Pty Ltd
Monticello is a vehicle to promote the pipeline project. It will establish the company, arrange finance and pipeline and terminal construction. After completion, the company will be floated to allow shareholding by Papua New Guineans.

Monticello Enterprises Pty Ltd (ME) has been formed by a small group of Papua New Guinea entrepreneurs, to pursue an alternative approach to the ownership of the pipeline. The basic purpose of the company is to establish a pipeline transmission company – to be named PNG Pipeline Company (PPC) – to own the initial pipeline and terminal facilities for the Kutubu Project, and to provide similar facilities for future petroleum developments.

4 PNG Pipeline Company
At least 51 percent of shares will be held by citizens and national institutions. Concessional finance and export credits can be obtained.

The funding of PPC would be footed on "user-pay" tolling contracts with the Kutubu Joint Venture companies. PPC would provide pipeline and terminal transmission services for the export of crude oil, without itself owning the export oil at any stage.

– Not less than 26 percent of the shares to be in the hands of Papua New

Guinea corporations and individuals, including provision for beneficial ownership of blocks of shares by customary title landholders along the right-of-way of the pipeline,
- 25 percent of the shares to be in the hands of one or more supranational institutions, such as IFC (International Finance Corporation) or CDC (Commonwealth Development Corporation), with provision for such shareholdings to be sold to Papua New Guinea investors by private placement or public issue some three to five years after the start-up of the project, and
- Not more than 49 percent to be in the hands of international institutional or corporate investors, some of which may also become similarly localised at a later date.

Sources of debt funding are likely to include:
- Officially supported export credits from the countries from which equipment, materials and construction services are purchased,
- IFC or CDC, related to their equity subscriptions, and
- International commercial banks.

5 Commercial relations with the Kutubu joint venture
Chevron will have technical and operational management of the pipeline.

Given the practicalities of the Kutubu Joint Venture, and the advanced state of project planning, we consider it essential that the Joint Venture be nominated by PPC as the implementing agency for the construction of the facilities. Thus, the Operator for the Joint Venture (Chevron) would be responsible for implementing the construction and commissioning of the facilities on behalf of PPC. Likewise, the Operator for the Joint Venture would be responsible for technical operation of the facilities under contract, on behalf of PPC, at least until such time as PPC were able to assume this function.

However, responsibility for executive management of PPC, and for monitoring of contractual performance of the construction and operation of the facilities, would remain with the board of PPC.

Similar contractual assignments of responsibilities have been invoked in the past in this country – for example, by the government to OTML (Ok Tedi Mining Limited) for the construction of the Kiunga Tabubil road, and by OTML to BHP Mining for mine operations – and in many other countries.

We believe that such contract management arrangements would be essential to ensure active co-operation from Chevron and its co-venturers in the Kutubu Joint Venture.

The transmission of oil through the pipeline and the export terminal would be undertaken by PPC as a service under a tolling contract. In order to secure the debt funding for PPC, the contract would necessarily be "user-pay", based on a minimum contractual throughput of oil. The Joint Venturers – including, if appropriate, the state – would retain title to the oil at all times, until title passed to the purchasers of the oil.

6 Benefits to Papua New Guinea

Expressed qualitatively, the benefits to Papua New Guinea are likely to include:
- the immediate and long term benefits to the state of a *common carrier* company;
- an enhanced degree of *national ownership*, particularly when additional equity is made available for public issue after operations have commenced;
- provision for *equity* by customary title *landholders*;
- more *beneficial* terms of some *debt facilities*, notably any provided by institutions such as IFC or CDC, with corresponding benefits to the national current account and balance of payments;
- *enhanced revenue* to the state, derived from:
- more rapid retirement of the state's "accumulated liability", and therefore earlier onset of receipts of the proceeds from oil sales,
- more rapid onset of Additional Profits Tax.

The incremental Petroleum Tax and Additional Profits Tax derived from the Joint Venture would be partially offset by the reduction in tax receipts flowing from the intrinsically less profitable pipeline and terminal operations of PPC.

7 Benefits to the oil companies

Expressed qualitatively, the benefits to oil companies are likely to include:
- greatly *reduced* requirements for *equity contributions*,
- correspondingly, *reduced* requirements for *debt obligations*, flowing from the translation of a large capital cost into an operating cost,

– *enhanced after-tax return* on funds employed, despite an incremental tax burden.

The oil companies would acquire these benefits, without losing technical control over the construction and operation of the facilities.

Although the Joint Venturers would have to provide minimum throughput undertakings to PPC (and its lenders), the undertakings are unlikely to be qualitatively different from or more onerous than those required for their own financing of the pipeline and terminal facilities, within the scope of an integrated project.

8 Likely reactions of Kutubu joint venture partners

The Joint Venture will argue that separation of the pipeline from oil production will
a delay project implementation,
b reduce their control of integrated project facilities,
c diminish their ability to raise debt capital as the PNG company would not be well known to international bankers.

Answers
a *There is no reason for material delay.* The two projects – pipeline and production – are totally interdependent. Since the Joint Venture will be responsible for constructing the pipeline and terminal on behalf of PPC, there should be no interruption to their current development plans and implementation timetable. The Joint Venture should sell at cost all pipeline-related technical studies completed to date to PPC.
b Since the Joint Venture will operate and manage the pipeline, *the risk of their loss of control damaging the project and their investment is immaterial.*
c Because the pipeline and production projects are interdependent, *bankers will view the two projects together in terms of financing.*

9 Conclusion

A decision must be made now by NEC to separate pipeline ownership from the Kutubu Joint Venture production project, otherwise it will be too late. *The proposal should be supported as it will allow greater PNG participation in the petroleum industry.*

Appendix 11

A chance for real PNG involvement in the oil industry

A personal rejoinder by Mr Mekere Morauta, one of the promoters of Monticello Enterprises Pty Ltd, to the Department of Minerals and Energy and Chevron Niugini.[1]

Statements recently reported in the Press by the Department of Minerals and Energy and Chevron Niugini have grossly misrepresented the proposal of an independent PNG-owned pipeline.

The first thing to be made clear is that the promoters of Monticello are not proposing to own the pipeline themselves. Monticello is merely a corporate vehicle established by a group of concerned Papua New Guineans, to promote the concept which would allow majority national ownership of an independent common carrier pipeline.

We saw an excellent opportunity for landowners, provincial governments and any other interested Papua New Guineans to become involved in our own developing oil industry in a meaningful way.

The second misrepresentation is that we have just dreamt up this idea at the last moment and are creating a hiccup in the process of approving the Kutubu project and getting it started. [The Department of] Minerals and Energy must admit that our proposal was put to them and the Department of Finance around the middle of last year. They were urged by the Prime Minister and their respective Ministers to advise the government on the merits or otherwise of the proposal, but to date have deliberately failed to have any serious discussions with or to provide any substantive advice to the government.

Many months ago we also met with Chevron to inform them of our proposal and to seek their cooperation in assessing its viability and impact on the project as a whole.

However, we came up against a brick wall, both with Chevron, and with expatriate bureaucrats.

We are concerned that some expatriates in Minerals and Energy seem to be very close to the very companies whose development proposals they are supposed to evaluate. If this is the case, we question whether these people are safeguarding the government's and national interests. It is the job of these bureaucrats to advise government on the widest aspects of resource development, not to represent foreign companies.

The present uncertainty is the result of the incompetence of these bureaucrats and their unwillingness to assess our proposals well before Chevron submitted the Kutubu Petroleum Development Project proposal. This is despite the fact that political leaders in our presence directed them to set up an inter-departmental committee to work with us to evaluate our proposal and advise the government accordingly. Minerals and Energy instead waited until two weeks ago, when they panicked and leaked our proposal to the Press.

We attempted to do everything the right way, through the proper channels. We expected cooperation from the public servants, and hoped for it from Chevron. Instead we have been ignored, denounced as "carpetbaggers" and taken as amateurs.

The essence of our proposal is that the pipeline and terminal facilities would not be owned solely by the Kutubu Joint Venture companies but by a separate company. This would allow Papua New Guinean ownership and would also ensure future producers access to the pipeline on open commercial terms. This will greatly increase the chances of other petroleum developments becoming a reality.

We are merely promoters of a corporate vehicle which will arrange finance and construction of the pipeline and terminal facilities. This company will be floated to enable landowners, provincial governments and any other Papua New Guinean who wishes to invest in this strategic national asset and resource development to do so. We have no intention now or ever of solely owning the pipeline company. We thought the little experience and expertise we have as individuals could be put together to achieve what we believe to be a project of great importance to Papua New Guinea. Successful development of the oil industry in a way which maximises benefits to Papua New Guineans has the potential to transform the social and economic well being of our young country.

We have done all in our power to avoid putting the government and the nation under pressure to make decisions about the pipeline. It is the pussyfooting and conniving of the bureaucrats which now result in their putting pressure on the government to make a decision in favour of foreign interests.

A third point of misrepresentation is that separating ownership of the pipeline from the Kutubu Joint Venture will delay the project. There is no need for any material delay if the Joint Venture and Minerals and Energy cooperate.

The projects go hand in hand. We are well prepared to assume responsibility for the pipeline aspect. The Joint Venture will be paid for all work done to date relating to the pipeline which should be made available to the PNG Pipeline Company.

The opportunity Papua New Guineans have now to have meaningful participation in this very strategic industry should not be missed without proper consideration. That is all we are asking the government. We want to urge the public servants to change their attitudes and, for once, exercise their imagination and take on some challenges.

This is our country and we Papua New Guineans should be leading it. The role of expatriate bureaucrats is to be good technical advisors. They are not here as foreign passengers to steer the boat and make decisions for us. When the boat sinks, we will be the ones who will go down with it.

The lessons of Bougainville should not be forgotten. Papua New Guineans are no longer satisfied with indirect benefits from resource developments. The resources belong to the nation; the land belongs to individuals, families and clans. Our people want to have direct beneficial ownership of and participation in these developments. State equity is no longer seen by a landowner in Kikori or Kutubu as an acceptable substitute for his own participation.

An independent pipeline company is a concrete example of how we might turn these aspirations into reality and meaningful commercial participation in the petroleum industry.

Note appendix 11

1   Article was an open letter published in the *Post Courier,* Papua New Guinea, on 7 May 1990.

Appendix 12

Fragile investor confidence and a nation's interest, by *John Millett*[1]

> "The lessons of Bougainville should not be forgotten. Papua New Guineas are no longer satisfied with indirect benefits from resource developments. The resources belong to the nation; the land belongs to individuals, families and clans. Our people want to have direct beneficial ownership of and participation in those developments. State equity is no longer seen by a landowner in Kikori or Kutubu as an acceptable substitute for his own participation."
>
> *Mr Mekere Morauta, Post Courier, May 7.*

Generally speaking, the shareholder's role is onerous. The shareholder is the first in line to contribute to a project and the last in line to participate in its benefits.

The shareholders' up-front equity contribution is the key to financing a project. Without it, banks will not lend to the project, the project will not proceed and the resource will remain latent in the ground.

On the other hand, the project must meet many obligations before it can reward shareholders with dividends on their equity subscription.

Employees must be paid, as must suppliers and contractors. Various taxes must be paid to governments. The resource-owner expects to receive royalties. Interest on loans must be paid and the loans repaid on schedule.

Only when all of these obligations have been met can the shareholder expect to be considered. Even then, the shareholders, through their elected board, must decide how much of the profit earned needs to be reinvested in the project before dividends can be distributed.

Much time can elapse after shareholders subscribe equity before they receive dividends. Ok Tedi, explored during the early '70s, has not yet paid an ordinary dividend. Oil Search has been exploring for oil in PNG for a great many years; but shareholders have not yet received a dividend.

Why, in these risky circumstances, is there clamour from Papua New Guineans to be shareholders in major projects? Economic nationalism would come first to mind as the principal reason.

This appears to be the basis of the Monticello proposal as explained by Mr Morauta. But this is not to say that economic pragmatism does not have a place in PNG today.

Two examples demonstrate that it has an important place. The Misima landowners have indicated that they prefer infrastructure to shares in the operating company. The second example relates to the Placer float in which many subscribers sold their allotments for solid capital gains rather than hold a stake in two of the country's most recent resource developments, Misima and Porgera.

Thus economic nationalism and economic pragmatism co-exist in PNG. National government's resource policies lean towards pragmatism on the grounds that the national interest can be maximised through fiscal policies rather than shareholding.

This preference is eminently sensible given that foreign investors are prepared to invest in resource development but not in other things that PNG needs badly, viz. basic education and health services and infrastructure, these being [the] government's responsibilities.

Mr Ramoi, Member for Aitape-Lumi, has advocated a statistic-approach to economic nationalism. The state would own the operating company and give a significant equity share (25-30 percent) to the landowners.

In the Monticello proposal, by contrast, private citizens, not the state, would be the entrepreneurs and, presumably, everybody would pay for their shares in the normal commercial manner.

These very different proposals have nonetheless been proposed to avoid the same problem, viz. "the Bougainville situation". But, are the events of the past 18 months in the North Solomons sufficiently well understood to be able to inform us of what ownership structures should apply to future resource developments? Were those events simply about ownership? About economic nationalism? It seems that, at least, ethnic factors played a part as did inter-generational and political power-sharing ones.

NIDA is [the] government's main instrument in promoting economic nationalism. It is the authority which, in general, determines where foreign investment is sought by PNG and where it is prohibited.

These demarcations are mainly based on economic sectors. For example, small-scale retailing and transport services have long been seen as sectors in which foreign capital, technology and expertise are not required. On the other hand, NIDA sees these foreign inputs as necessary to develop the mining and petroleum sectors.

Paradoxically perhaps, some citizens who enjoy the protection from foreign competition provided by NIDA, break the prohibition by inviting foreign participation in their ventures.

Whether it is capital, technology or expertise that the citizen wants from his foreign partner is not clear. It could be all three, the local partner being happy to collect the economic rent created by the protection afforded by the state.

Within the NIDA framework, itself under review, economic development has moved the demarcation boundary to encompass a wider range of sectors restricted to PNG ownership. For example, the view has been expressed that all retailing and wholesaling should be included in NIDA's restricted activities. If shortage of domestic capital is the reason for unintended foreign involvement in the smaller retailing sector, then it would be a much bigger constraint were the whole of the retailing and wholesale sectors to be reserved. Likewise, the economic rents created would be commensurately bigger.

The extraction and distribution of petroleum is an international industry which PNG has aspired for 70 years to join. The oil price hikes of the 1970s created an impetus for PNG to make itself attractive to international oil exploration capital.

The state developed policies and took them and promoted them in the headquarters of the world's oil majors. Their policies and promotion have succeeded in that the state now has before it an application to develop an oil field in the Southern Highlands Province.

The oil would flow by pipeline to an ocean terminal in the Gulf of Papua. Under existing policies the pipeline would be an integral part of the oil field with no separation of ownership.

The Monticello proposal seeks to separate ownership of the pipeline from that of the oil field on the grounds that by so doing all Papua New Guineans can participate more meaningfully in this new development.

While creating assets is onerous, particularly for shareholders, ownership of assets offers the potential for psychological as well as financial rewards. Great buildings have brought their owners much pleasure and prestige throughout the ages. In all cultures, in this tradition the recent opening of the first high-rise building in Mt. Hagen must have been a moment of immense pride to its owners. For landlords, their architectural creations are the source of the psychological reward from their investment. Farmers, the bulk of Papua New Guineans, no doubt also enjoy a sense of pride in seeing their crops grow healthy and strong as a result of their labours. What similar benefits might flow to owners of an oil pipeline?

In PNG we have nothing to go on since we don't yet have one. But one expects that it would be mostly buried and not available for visual enjoyment. Nor would it provide much employment. Benefits would be surely financial.

What do Investment Corporation of PNG, Minerals Resource Development Company, the Placer float, the Highlands Gold float and Monticello have in common? A purpose – to provide a means for Papua New Guineans to have a financial interest in companies operating in PNG.

They differ as to ownership. ICPNG and MRDC are government authorities. Placer and Highlands Gold are foreign-owned companies. Monticello is private national-owned although it envisages shareholding by provincial governments.

Thus, as well as the Monticello proposal, a number of alternatives suggest themselves to provide for a broad-based financial stake in this emergent industry. A public issue in the overall development, or a placement to ICPNG or MRDC. If ownership is to be separated, ICPNG or MRDC might be suitable vehicles.

The bonafides of the Monticello principals are beyond question. They have all served PNG well and true and continue in their respective and complementary fields of expertise to do so. But if they are not to own the company which owns the pipeline as they have stated to be the case, then who will own it?

This question must concern both the developers of the oil field and the state. As a public company, what restrictions will apply to share transfers? Could control of the pipeline pass to foreign interests, defeating Monticello's basic purpose in the same way that NIDA's purpose is subverted? Could the developer face the situation after having put in all the hard work of finding and developing the oil field, of having to bargain with a competitor who has gained control of the pipeline?

Investor confidence is a fragile thing. It is strengthened by constancy and predictability of policy. Separate ownership of the pipeline – a change in the rules of the game – whether by a state or a private monopoly may well be a blessing 'in disguise' for the developer and the state – possible insurance against a future 'Bougainville'.

But it is not a guaranteed insurance. It is a question therefore of risk evaluation. Separate ownership would pose a whole new risk environment which would take time to evaluate. And the delay itself would introduce further risks.

Note appendix 12
1   John Millet is the Executive Director of the Institute of National Affairs. This article was published in the *Post Courier* of Papua New Guinea on 11 May 1990.

Appendix 13

Economic nationalism and foreign capital, an opinion by *J. J. Tauvasa*[1]

The debate over national participation in the development and ownership of strategic economic assets has drawn much publicity recently, in the case of the ownership of the oil pipeline. Critics of the concept initiated by the group of national individuals who are advocating for the separate ownership of this asset to be largely in the hands of Papua New Guineans, denounces the idea as being rent seeking, discouraging foreign investment, and inconsistent with current legislation. Supporters, for nationalistic reasons, maintain that ownership of vital economic infrastructure enhances greater participation in the direction and destiny of the country's economy.

As a proponent of the latter school of thought, I am unavoidably drawn into the debate of the ownership of the oil pipeline, because of my interest in contributing to, and achievement of some degree of balance between foreign investment and national equity in our economy and enterprise. The views expressed in this dissertation over these two elements of development are personal, and are not the official position of professional organisations that I represent.

Too often we hear those who evaluate Papua New Guinea as a place for investments refer to issues such as the lack of infrastructure, business management, and technical skills as critical impediments to development. It would be misleading of me to say that Papua New Guinea does not have these fundamental economic and commercial concerns.

I mention these development criteria here because these issues are causing some of us who are concerned about the peripheral multiplier association offered to the trustees of resources and national entrepreneurs from development projects, to suggest options for greater involvement, and therefore improve the position of PNG to future evaluation.

It is ironical to note that fifteen years after independence, the only substantive economic acclamation we make is that we have been able to successfully manage our economy. Observation however, suggests that in spite of this proclamation, PNG's economy by and large is owned and controlled by someone else.

Economic Nationalism

I do not think that this situation should continue nor do I believe that our political masters should condone their position as being purely managers of the economy. Evidently there is a nationalistic urge expressed by way of demands for compensation or participation by landowners, provincial governments, national companies and individuals in economic opportunities. This urge is an intangible force driving many to a cash environment, from subsistence economy in the rural communities, and small business operations in urban centres. This is the wave of economic nationalism, which believe it or not, is here to stay unless structural socio-economic adjustments are promulgated to ease the tensions.

My colleague Mr Mekere Morauta in his recent article [*Post Courier*, 7 May 1990, PD] explicitly referred to it as ... "our people want to have direct beneficial ownership in the developments". Already there is a degree of participation and ownership in developments through corporate institutions such as the Investment Corporation of PNG and Highlands Gold Limited. This distinction in investment by citizens in state-owned corporation and private sector organisations was also drawn by Mr John Millett of the Institute of National Affairs on his commentary on economic nationalism. [*Post Courier*, 11 May 1990, PD]

It is to be noted that in this environment, where the government is the scenario builder, pre-determining the conditions for development, the urge for greater participation in the economy is bound to rise further. In fact, the mere existence of foreign-owned and controlled enterprises, which essentially govern the country's economic performance, pose yet another cause for economic nationalism. This is in spite of the level of investment made by the companies concerned.

Unfortunately some of our people seem to be convinced that we are now better off because of our ownership of PMVs, trade stores, and smallholder agricultural blocks. I do not believe that this position enhances our aspiration for a balanced ownership of our economy, moreover, a say in its direction. Economic nationalism means more than that. Political leaders, government advisors, and concerned public, have to think beyond this limitation. It means ownership, control and participation in larger scale economic development. Let me qualify this by saying that it does not mean nationalisation of businesses.

In advancing greater participation in the development of our economic infrastructure, the promoters of economic nationalism are now accused of self-interest, and destabilising the path towards attracting foreign capital, and investment.

Even uninformed critics seem to suddenly become well versed in national issues and sought to undermine the integrity of the concerned individuals who over the years have sweated for PNG. I have deliberately implied political sentiments in defining economic nationalism because they are fundamental aspects of the Eight Point Plan which was, and I believe still is, the economic manifesto of the government.

Rules of the Game

Just over two decades ago when political nationalism was advocated by Sir Michael Somare and his "Bully Beef" club, they were verbally tormented and critics denounced them as being naive to even contemplate that Papua New Guineans could manage their own political affairs. Of course, at that time, there was very little commentary from the rural population as most people were not aware of the wave of political aspiration in the country. Despite this, the political wishes of the few were convincing enough to sway Konedobu [the then seat of Administration, ed.] and Canberra to grant self-determination to PNG in 1973 followed by political independence in 1975.

I have drawn this analogy because the issue of ownership of the oil pipeline characterises a similar "David and Goliath" story, in which the issue at stake is no longer political nationalism but rather economic nationalism. Only this time, the umpire is the government, and the players are, a corporate multi national versus a group of concerned individuals. As to who wins, its anyone's guess.

At an investment seminar held in Brisbane during Expo '88, I stated in a paper designed to entice foreign capital into PNG that in spite of foreign capital being accustomed to working with a full spectrum of political ideologies, it needs to be able to depend on rules to stay constant over long periods. Stability is more important than ideology.

What I did not say at this seminar was that most investment and development rules applied in PNG today were established pre self-government and independence. They could not have taken account of the rapidity and complexity of the changing circumstances, and indeed the changing attitudes of PNG citizens.

The "goal posts", a term commonly used by foreign capital to denote the rules, were designed to ensure that the favoured side with the resources to win the game, will always win.

This is the state of play that remains prevalent in the investment and development game in PNG. It is sad to see that political, bureaucratic and technical advice cannot suggest alternatives to development, in view of today's environment, but to maintain a position of applying the "easy way out" through the advocacy of not shifting the goal posts.

Foreign Capital

Let me reiterate the notion that foreign capital is accustomed to working with full spectrum of political ideologies, and that stability is more important than ideology. Throughout the 1980s, investment in private mining and non-mining sectors of the economy grew, averaging fifty-six percent of the gross domestic product. This rate of growth was attained despite the existence of varying political ideologies and instability.

Foreign capital is attracted to PNG primarily because the resources for development are here; and that compared to similar resource endowed countries, the short and long term risks associated with investments are generally less.

Additionally, there is no doubt that the controls exercised by the PNG government in respect of the conditions of entry, the operation of the foreign developer, the remittances of profits and repatriation of capital, would at one stage or other have been discussed at board levels to determine (if any) further injection or contribution of capital into the country.

One must admit that concessions granted by the country, notwithstanding the downside of the socio-political environment perpetuated by continued security to property, civil strife, and criminal activities, have provided incentive to foreign capital.

What is disconcerting now is the view that the proposal by a group of national citizens to allow the public at large to be involved in part of the economic development process by foreign capital, would destabilise PNG's investment climate. Such a view is held predominantly by foreign companies who invariably show dissatisfaction at the lack of attendance by national executives at seminars and meetings. Yet they adopt in a most suppressive way any constructive proposal designed to facilitate greater national participation. I have highlighted this small example, because it epitomises the very unbalanced nature of the private sector and enterprise in this country.

The country's exposure to economic and technological changes, and the peoples' changing attitudes to their social well being must instill an appreciation that fifteen years of investment stability governed by pre-independence rules, is relatively a long time. It may be timely now for the adjudicators and umpires of the game to amend the rules for long term stability and achievement of the balance referred to earlier.

The positive effect of this move is that, local equity participation from the start of developing an economic infrastructure could minimise the country's exposure to one hundred percent foreign capital inflow, if the use of domestic savings are applied. More importantly, it allows a subsequent positive distribution effect into the economy from retained profits earned by the local investors.

But economic nationalism is unattainable when foreign capital elects to exclude local partnership because of its corporate policy, or it becomes unattractive to engage local equity for some other reasons.

Conclusion

Let me draw the conclusions of this dissertation and refer specifically to the issue at hand; Chevron and the joint venture Partners versus Monticello. In doing so, I am mindful of these three factors:

1. It is not unusual in the petroleum industry worldwide for the transmission utility or oil pipeline to be owned by those other than developers of the oil reserves. Examples of joint venture ownerships exist in Continental Western Europe.
2. Monticello will NOT own, or ever will own the pipeline. PNG Pipeline Company which is being proposed to own this vital strategic economic asset will have substantial Papua New Guinea equity.
3. Chevron and the JBP have spent considerable funds in the exploration and feasibility study towards the production of the Iagifu oil field. And, under existing Legislation the company has advantage over Monticello's proposal.

Foreign capital is welcomed in PNG. External inputs to developing our natural resources is now more imminent than ever before. But if we are to believe that foreign capital is accustomed to working with a full spectrum of political ideologies and would like to see long term stability in investment, then foreign investors should be comfortable with local partners who can contribute to the enterprise. The establishment of long term association, equity capital and local knowledge are substantive contributions to the investment project.

It is a fact that neither Monticello nor any other locally owned investor has spent any funds in the quest for oil in this country. It is also a fact that the government and people of PNG are trustees of the resources of their land. The latter view represents a political ideology, whilst the former characterises the financial predicaments of national investors caused by the country's development process.

The wave of economic nationalism is real and should not be discarded by foreign capital. Joint venture ownership of investment projects between local and foreign interests is not an unnecessary evil. Because it is being perceived as disruptive to the investment climate and a deterrent to further foreign capital, many citizens who are conscious of the pace of economic development, but are unable to initiate greater participation in the spin-off effects, are not comforted by the notion that Papua New Guineans should not be involved.

The umpire (the government) has to weigh the strengths and merits of enforcing existing outdated laws to settle the apparent dispute of economic nationalism versus foreign capital. Foremost in the government's agenda should be its responsibility to the practical application of its economic manifesto, and maintaining long term investment stability.

Participation, ownership and control of the economy and enterprise are meaningless unless we start somewhere.

Perhaps the starting point would be for discussions between all parties, government, Chevron, and Monticello to identify options mutually satisfactory to all.

Note appendix 13

1   Joe Tauvasa is a promotor of the Monticello Proposal and is a Principal of Pacific Tankships Pty Ltd. This article was published in the *Post Courier* of Papua New Guinea in May 1990.

Appendix 14

PNG Mining & Petroleum Projects[1]

Many exploration licences are issued and renewed every year by the Government of Papua New Guinea. Exploration licences for minerals are issued for a period of two years and can be renewed. Licences for hydrocarbon exploration are issued for a period of six years at a time and can be renewed also. Interests in licences can be bought or sold at costs. The following is a resume of the existing mines and the potential projects of the future.

1   Bougainville Mine

It has been closed since 1989. At time of publication the Government is reported to be in control of the mine site as well as of 90% of the island of Bougainville. At time of its closure it was reported to have reserves of 496 million tonnes having the grades of 0.42% copper and 0.55 grams of silver per tonne. 53.6% of the mine is owned by CRA and the PNG Government owns 19.1%. There has been an embargo against exploration in adjacent areas for some time.

The landowners had no reserved interests in this mine.

2   Ok Tedi Mine

BHP owns 30% of the mine. Recently, it has been reported that AMOCO (30%) will sell its interests to PNG Government and BHP. The PNG Government owns 20% but is likely to increase its interests with AMOCO's sellout. The German consortium of Metallgesellschaft, DEG and Degussa owned 20%. It is likely that with a corporate restructuring Metallgesellschaft will acquire the interests of the other two German entities and place all its copper interests under its subsidiary the Metall Mining Corporation of Canada. The reserves are placed at 1.2 million tonnes of gold ore, 51.04

million tonnes of skarn, 420.6 million tonnes of sulphide copper and 14.5 million tonnes of oxide copper. Exploration is being undertaken in adjacent areas.

The landowners have no direct shareholding in this mine.

3 Porgera Mine

Major interests of this gold mine is divided between Placer (25%), Highlands Gold (25%) and Renison Goldfields Consolidated (25%). The PNG Government owns 20.1%. This is both an underground gold and an open pit mine. The ore reserves are placed at 85.8 million tonnes with grades of 24.5 grams of gold per tonne in underground and 5.7 grammes of gold per tonne for the open pit and 11.9 grammes of silver per tonne.

The landowners have a minor interest of 2.45% in this mine.

4 Misima Mine

This mine is located on the island of Misima. It is owned by Placer (80%) and PNG Government (20%). Its reserves are placed at 40 million tonnes of ore with 1.25 grammes of gold per tonne and 14.1 grammes of silver per tonne.

The landowners have no interest in this mine.

5 Mt Kare Alluvial Gold Mine & Hard Rock Deposit

CRA withdrew its operations from the mine after a difficult dispute with the landowners and the licensee for the alluvial gold mining operations is now a company organised by the landowners themselves. CRA was to retain its licence for the hard rock deposit but in January 1992, the mining camp was invaded by the landowners resulting in the destruction of buildings and a helicopter. CRA has now withdrawn from this licence area.

6 Hides Gas Field

British Petroleum owns 95% of the field. It is estimated to contain a minimum of 2.31 trillion cubic feet of gas. It has a small facility to produce sales gas, naphtha and diesel and suuplies a 30 Mw of electricity to the Porgera gold mine.

The landowners have no reserved interest in this gas field.

7 Kutubu Oil Project

The oil field is owned by several companies some of which are Chevron

(19.37%), British Petroleum (19.37%), BHP Petroleum (9.69%), Ampolex (11.61%), and the PNG Government at (22.5%). It has a proven reserve of 215 million barrels of oil recoverable with about 1.8 trillion cubic feet of gas which is being re-injected.

The debate reproduced in Appendices 10, 11, 12 and 13 were in respect to whether or not the Government of Papua New Guinea should grant a pipeline licence to Chevron and the interest holders of the oil field. The proponents of the Monticello proposal (as it became to be known and highlighted in Part B of this book) urged the Government to grant the pipeline licence to an independent pipeline company shares in which are to be made available for public subscription by Papua New Guineans with a certain percentage reserved for the landowners of the pipeline route.

The landowners of both the oil field and the pipeline route have no reserved interest in the oil field and the pipeline respectively.

8 Hidden Valley Prospect

The exploration licence holder is CRA Minerals Pty Ltd. The estimated ore reserves are placed at 49 million tonnes with grades of 1.8 grammes of gold pe tonne and 24.0 gammes of silver per tonne.

9 Lihir Prospect

This is a gold deposit on Lihir island. The licensees are Kennecott and Niugini Mining. It is an epithermal, oxide and sulphide gold ore deposit. The deposit is estimated at 103.98 million tonnes of ore with grades at 4.37 gammes of gold per tonne. It is reported that RTZ will reduce its interests through Kennecott and additional funds will be aised for the project through a possible public float co-sponsored by the PNG Government.

The landowners have successfully negotiated a 20% interest in this project.

10 South East Gobe Oil Prospect

The larger interest holders of this oil field are Southern Highland Petroleum Co. (50.5%) Barracuda (20%) and Oil Search Limited (20%). Current discoveries place the estimated reserves at about 100 million barrels. Further exploration activities are being conducted.

11 Tolukuma Prospect

The licensee is Dome Resources N.L. which is 100% owned by Newmont.

It is an epithermal quartz vein gold deposit. Its reserves are estimated at 1.4 million tonnes of ore with grades of 12.41 grammes of gold per tonne and which includes 440,000 tonnes at 17 grammes of gold per tonne and 46 grammes of silver per tonne.

12 Tabar Prospect
This is located at Tabar island. The licensees are Kennecott Australia (63%), Nord Pacific (29%) and Niugini Mining (8%). This is an epithermal gold and silver prospect. Its estimated reserves are 695,000 tonnes of oxide only containing 4.21 gammes of gold per tonne.

13 Wafi Prospect
The licensee is CRA. It is an epithermal (acid-sulphate) gold and porphyry copper deposit. Estimated reserves are not known.

14 Wapolu Prospect
The licensees are Union Mining (51%) and Mac Mining (49%). This is an epithermal gold deposit in a volcanic dome. It is located on Fergusson island. Its estimated reseves are placed at 1.9 million tonnes of ore with grades at 2.4 grammes of gold per tonne.

15 Woodlark Island Prospect
The licensee is Highlands Gold. The deposit is described as gold with pyrite and base metal quartz veins in altered volcanics. The reserves are estimated at 2.2 million tonnes with grades at 3.41 grammes of gold per tonne of ore.

Note appendix 14
1   Source: Department of Mining and Petrolem, July to September 1993, *Quarterly Report*.

Notes

A Indigenous or Aboriginal Rights to Property: A Papua New Guinea Perspective

1. Margaret Mead: *Sex and Temperament in Three Primitive Societies.*
2. See publications under Books and Materials section of the Bibliography.
3. Total land area is 47,615,700 hectares of which 1,305,281 hectares (2.75%) are owned by the state and 46,310,419 hectares (97.25%) are owned by the indigenous landowners. *PNG Law Reform Commission Monograph,* No. 5, "Land Law and Policy in Papua New Guinea", p. 33.
4. The Mining Industry of Papua New Guinea relies on the opinion of Posman Kisokiu, a Papua New Guinean lawyer who is a partner of an Australian based law firm, which opinion is based on the fiction of Crown rights. Andrew Corren, another Papua New Guinean lawyer then in the employ of Bougainville Copper Limited presented a paper entitled, "Compensation for Damage to Land as a Result of Mining Operations" at the PNG Law Society Conference in 1989 wherein he was bold enough to state, "Because the property in gold and mineral resources has always been vested in the state, no acquisition of an interest in or right over property and no compulsory taking of possession of property is prohibited by the constitution". This reasoning is no longer valid in Australia following the recent Australian High Court ruling in the Eddie Mabo's case [(1992) 66 ALJR No. 7, 408] in respect to ownership of Murray Island. In that case the High Court recognised that a form of native title exist where ownership of land had not been transferred by freehold sale.
5. *Post Courier* Report, 14 August 1992, p. 6.
6. The Bougainville mine has been closed since 1989 following an uprising by landowners.
7. CRA has decided to withdraw from its alluvial gold claim over Mt. Kare in the Enga Province, but not after substantial loss of capital equipment including one helicopter in landowner conflicts.

8   Survey conducted by *Australian Mining Journal* amongst selected mining and petroleum companies and published in Australia's *Mining Monthly*, February 1993. The survey was subsequently rejected by Robert Needham, the managing director of the Papua New Guinea government's Mineral Resources Development Company, in his article captioned "Survey Critique Points to Sound Democratic Record" in the April 1993 issue of Australia's Mining Monthly.
9   See Chapter IV, Part A of this book.
10 See Chapter IV and VI, Part A of this book.
11 The gold rush into the Wau and Bulolo areas of New Guinea in the 1930s was effected on traditional land and not on land which had been purchased by the Administering authority. The landowners of the Wau and Bulolo gold fields or at least their descendants may have a claim against the Australian government for breach of trust under the League of Nations Mandate under which it administered New Guinea after the first world war.
12 Commodore Erskine's Proclamation of the Protectorate over Papua in 1884 and the Imperial Charter for the German Neu Guinea Kompagnie of 17th May 1885 reproduced in this book as Appendix 1 and Appendix 2.
13 See note 4 above, where the exception is the recent Eddie Mabo's case which recognised native title in Australia.
14 New Guinea Collection, University of Papua New Guinea: "The History of Papua New Guinea, Commodore Erskine's Proclamation" published in a supplement to the *Queensland Government Gazette* on 23rd December 1884. Great Britain, House of Commons, Sessional Papers Vol. LIV (1884-1885), C. – 4217, Encl. 1 in No. 148, p. 122, reproduced in this book as Appendix 1.
15 See Appendix 1.
16 O'Connell, D.P. and Ann Riordan, *Opinions on Imperial Constitutional Law*, Australian Law Book Company Ltd, 1971, p. 417.
17 Ibid, p. 418.
18 Op cit p. 419.
19 Dr. John Mugambwa, "Land Disputes in PNG: A Colonial Legacy and Post Independence Solutions", (1987) 15 *MLJ* 94 at p. 96.
20 Cf. Professor R.W. James, "Land Law and Policy in Papua New Guinea", *Law Reform Commission Monograph* No. 5, on page 142 where he explained that wholesale confiscation was justified by the theory that the legal title to the land was automatically vested in the colonisers and that land rights of indigenous people were encumbrances (licenses) on that title which can be revoked at any time by the Administrators and at their will. See Paper by John Hookey, "The

Contribution of the Supreme Court to the Recognition of Customary Rights in Land", Seventh Waigani Seminar publication on Law and Development, University of Papua New Guinea; See also *Tee-Hit-Ton Indians v. US* (1955) 348 US 272; *Milirrpum v. Nabalco Pty Ltd* (1971) 17 FLR 141; *Williams v. AG of New South Wales* (1913) 16 CLR 404; *Calder v. AG of British Colombia* (1971) 13 DLR (3rd) 80.

21 D.K.G., Vol. 1, 434-6; interpreted and reproduced in *The Land Law of German New Guinea* by Peter and Bridget Sack, Australian National University 1975, p. 1. See Appendix 2.
22 Ibid, p. 5. See Appendix 3.
23 (1950) ICJ 128 at p. 149 [Advisory Opinion on International Status of South West Africa (Namibia)].
24 ICJ op cit, p. 149.
25 Ibid, p. 150.
26 Ibid, p. 152; (1937) 58 CLR 528 at pp. 552, 553.
27 (1950) ICJ 128 op cit, p. 152; (1937) 58 CLR 528 at pp. 581, 582.
28 The leading proponent of this theory in Papua New Guinea is Posman Kisokiu. This theory is relied upon by the Papua New Guinea Chamber of Mines and Petroleum, the government's Department of Mining and Petroleum and possibly by the Institute of National Affairs. This theory has now been rejected in New Zealand and recently in Australia, see note 4 above.
29 Article 17.
30 Article 1 of both Covenants.
31 Article 1, paragraph 10.
32 Ibid, paragraph 6.
33 Article 2.
34 Guest Speaker at a dinner organised by Kaltenbach & Voigt GmbH & Co. on 12th March 1993 at La Redoute, in Bad Godesberg – Bonn, Germany on the subject of "The Current Position of Germany within Europe".
35 Argument proffered by Dr. Otto von Habsburg.
36 See footnotes 14 & 15.
37 1823.
38 1832.
39 Personal conversation with Mich McWalters.
40 Section 35.
41 Henry Reynolds, *The Law of the Land,* p. 46, Penguin Books 1987.
42 Section 2 (2).
43 (1921) 2 AC 399.

44 Section 2(2) of PNG constitution.
45 Section 53 of PNG constitution.
46 Paragraphs 87 & 88 of Constitutional Planning Committee Report at p. 5/1/15.
47 Leroy Little Bear, "A Concept of Native Title", *CASNP Bulletin,* Dec 1976, p. 34.
48 (1939) AC 256.
49 Section 2(2).
50 Section 53.
51 See Appendix 6 of this book.
52 (1843) 152 ER 704.
53 Ibid, at p. 707.
54 (1855) 61 ER 883.
55 JRS Forbes & AG Lang, *Australian Mining & Petroleum Laws,* 2nd Edition, 1987 Butterworths, at p. 14.
56 (1848) 136 ER 987; ibid p. 14.
57 (1882) 20 Ch.D. 151, (1881) AII ER 585; ibid p. 14.
58 See list of selected American cases under various headings in the bibliography section of this book.
59 (1568) 75 ER 472.
60 (1960) AIR 1080.
61 (1960) AIR 1000.
62 'Minerals' is defined by the Mining Act as meaning all valuable non-living substances obtainable from land. The Mining Act also defined "land" as including the surface and any ground beneath the surface of the land; water; the foreshore; offshore seabed; bed of any river, stream, lake or swamp; and any interest in land. Section 5(1) of the Mining Act says:
> "All minerals existing on, in or below the surface of any land in Papua New Guinea, including any minerals contained in any water lying on any land in Papua New Guinea, are the property of the State."

Petroleum is defined by the Petroleum Act to mean any naturally occuring hydrocarbons, whether in a gaseous, liquid or solid state but does not include coal, shale or any substance which may be extracted from coal, shale or other rock.

Section 5 (1) of the Petroleum Act states:
> "Subject to this Act, but notwithstanding anything contained in any other law or in any other grant, instrument of title or other document, all petroleum and helium at or below the surface of any land is and shall be deemed at all times to have been, the property of the State."

63 (1989) 2 NZLR 513 at p. 520.

64 (1965) 2 All ER 547 at p. 555.
65 Section 102 of the Mining Act, Ch. No. 195; Equivalent provision in Petroleum Act.
66 See footnote 52.
67 Appendices 4, 5 and 6.
68 Reproduced in Appendix 8.
69 Paul Ehrlich, *The Population Bomb* 1971 at p. 104.
70 Robert Chambers, *Rural Development – Putting the Last First,* Longman Scientific and Technical, 1983, p. 161.
71 Chambers, op cit, pp. 163, 164.
72 New Guinea Collection, op cit. See footnotes 14, 15.

B Equality and Participation

1 *Premdas v. The State* (1979) PNGLR 329. This case involves the power of the Minister for Foreign Affairs in deportation proceedings. Nevertheless, Premdas was a lecturer in politics at the University of Papua New Guinea. He was alleged to be openly propagating marxist philosophies amongst young Papua New Guinean students at the University of Papua New Guinea. He was declared *persona non grata* by the government.

2 A.P. Power, "The Future of Clans in Papua New Guinea in the 21st Century", Paper delivered at the 17th Waigani Seminar and reproduced in Hughes & Thirlwall, *The Ethics of Development – Choices in Development Planning,* Vol. 4, *University of Papua New Guinea Press,* p. 156. At p. 157, Power pointed out that: *"If the clan does not survive the consequent social and economic disaggregation, with accompanying inequalities, this will cause significant social disruption, pulling Papua New Guinea down to the level of so many other developing countries."* The Seventh Directive Principle of the Second National Goal as stated in the constitution called for *"active steps to be taken to facilitate the organisation and legal recognition of all groups engaging in development activities".* The best method of recognising the traditional corporate structure is to give legal recognition to the clan structure together with its intricate decision-making process. In an effort to achieve that objective the Land Groups Incorporation Act was passed by parliament but to date no active steps have been taken by government to promote its utilisation both amongst Papua New Guineans and foreign investors.

3 Certain landowners of Mt. Kare, Porgera Gold mine, Hides Gas project and

Kutubu Oil fields have been branded as terrorists by the foreign company personnel and certain elements of government including our own politicians. Source: Personal conversations.

4   See note 2.
5   CRA has now decided to withdraw from the Mt. Kare alluvial claim on the condition that another Australian company, Ramsgate Resources Limited (which was alleged to be financing the legal costs of the dissident landowners), is not substituted for CRA. See also headline article captioned "Mt. Kare – Our New Bougainville !" in the *Times of Papua New Guinea* publication of 23 January 1992 and article captioned "CRA suspends operations at Mount Kare gold mine", *Post Courier,* 25 February 1993.
6   Survey conducted by the *Australian Mining Journal* and published in February 1993 issue of *Mining Monthly* rated Papua New Guinea at the bottom of all countries including USSR and Indonesia.
7   Mobil has extended its involvement in oil exploration in Papua New Guinea and has also brought some Japanese joint venture partners. The Malaysians and Singaporeans have moved positively towards Papua New Guinea with the announcement of investments in forestry and fisheries-related industries. The Koreans have moved into shipbuilding and cement works. The Americans are also keen in the fisheries area. This will auger well for Papua New Guinea. The new initiative of the Wingti Government to look north is intended to capitalise on the expanding growth area in the world. Papua New Guinea appears well advised to move in that direction. The Australian industries can only benefit if they change their current attitude and move positively to assist Papua New Guinea to restructure its economic base then to continue to pose obstacles.
8   Constitutional Planning Committee Report, paragraph 87, page 5/1/15.
9   Second National Goal, National Constitution.
10 Sixth Directive Principle of the Second National Goal, National Constitution.
11 Noreo Beangke, Managing Director of Credit Corporation (PNG) Limited, a Papua New Guinean finance company.
12 Frank Kramer, Chairman and Managing Director of Kinhill Kramer (PNG) Pty Limited, the largest Papua New Guinean engineering firm.
13 Joe Tauvasa, Chairman and Managing Director of Pacific Tankships Pty Ltd.
14 Warner Shand – Lawyers of Papua New Guinea.
15 HE Mr Robert Ferand (American Ambassador to PNG).
16 HE Mr Alan Taylor (Australian High Commissioner to PNG).
17 Lowan village, Wewak in East Sepik Province of Papua New Guinea.
18 Personal discussions with Sir Mekere Morauta.

19 Greg Anderson.
20 Sir Mekere Morauta was forced by the Ombudsman Commission to resign his post as the Executive Director of Burns Philp (PNG) Limited when he left the position of Secretary for Finance in the government of Papua New Guinea and took up that post, even though he had not at any time during his term in government dealt with that company in his official capacity.
21 Constitutional Planning Committee (CPC) Report, paragraph 66, page 2/9.
22 CPC Report, paragraph 73, page 2/9.
23 CPC Report, paragraph 109, page 5/1/17.
24 CPC Report, paragraph 110, pages 5/1/17-18.
25 Personal conversation with the Prime Minister.
26 At the time of publication, agreement had been reached to increase the government's participation to 25 percent.
27 Hernando de Soto, "The Missing Ingredient", *The Economist* of September 11th – 17th 1993, p. 10 of special publication commemorating *The Economist*'s 150 year anniversary.
28 Hernando de Soto, op cit, pp. 13-14.

Bibliography

Select bibliography of court cases

Possession
1. *Cooper v. Stuart* (1889) 14 AC 291
2. Gove Land Rights Case (1971) 17 Federal Law Reports 270
3. *Millirpum v. Nabalco* (1971) 17 Federal Law Reports 245 (141?)
4. *Williams v. Attorney General*, NSW, (1913) 16 Commonwealth Law Review 439
5. *Worcester v. Georgia* (1832)
6. *Tyson v. Smith* (1838)
7. *Falmouth v. George* (1828)
8. *Jones v. Williams* (1837) All ER 424
9. *Harper v. Charlesworth* (1825) All ER 66 at p. 68
10. *Lord Advocate v. Young* (1887) 12 AC 556
11. *Lord Advocate v. Lord Blantyne* (1879) 4 AC 770
12. *Chambers v. Donaldson* (1809) 103 ER 929
13. *Johnson v. Barret* 82 ER 887
14. *Clark v. Elphinstone* (1880) 6 AC 164
15. *Lord Advocate v. Lovat* (1880) 5 AC 273
16. *A-G v. Newcastle-upon-Tyne Corporation* (1895-9) All ER 747
17. *Hanbury v. Jenkins* (1901) 2 Ch. 401
18. *Ecroyd v. Coulthard* (1897) 2 Ch. 554
19. *Johnson v. O'Neil* (1911) AC 552

By what tenure
20. (1849) 4 & 5 Will, IV C. 95
21. *Wilson v. Terry* (1849)
22. *U.S. v. Pecheman* (1833)
23. *Dalton v. Angus* (1881) 6 AC 773
24. *White v. McLean* (1890) SA CASE

25 *Mitchell v. U.S.* (1835)
26 *Fletcher v. Peck* (1810)
27 *Johnson v. McIntosh* (1823)
28 *Cherokee Nation v. Georgia* (1834)
29 *Hamlet of Baker Lake v. Minister of Indian Affairs* (1980) 107 Dominion Law Review 513
30 *Calder v. Attorney General of British Colombia* (1973) 34 Dominion Law Review 203; (1970) 13 DLR (3d) 80
31 *R. v. Secretary of State* (1985) All ER 124
32 *Oyekan v. Adele* (1957) All ER 785 at p. 788
33 *Haoni Te Heuheu Tukino v. Aotea District Moari Land Board* (1941) 2 All ER 93; (1941) AC 308
34 *Amodu Tijani v. Southern Nigeria (Secretary)* (1921) 2 AC 399
35 *Sakariyawo Oshodi v. Moriamo Dakolo* (1930) AC 667
36 *Sunmonu v. Disu Raphael* (1927) AC 881
37 *Idewa Inosa v. Sakoriyawo Oshodi* (1934) AC 99
38 *Hemmings v. Stoke Poges Golf Club* (1920) AC

Presumption of constitutionality
39 *Minister for Home Affairs v. Bickle and Others* (1985) LRC (Const.) 755
40 *Jones v. Commonwealth of Australia* (1936) AC 578 at p. 613
41 *A-G v. Morgan* (1985) LRC (Const.) 770
42 *A-G v. Lawrence* (1985) LRC (Const.) 921
43 *Ukaegbu v. A-G of Imo State* (1985) LRC (Const.) 867

Reconnaisance and re-assessment
44 *Nireaha Tamaki v. Baker* (1901) AC 577

Land rights recognised
45 *Jones v. Meehan* (1899) 175 U.S. Law Reports 11
46 *New Windsor Corporation v. Mellor* (1975) (Privy Council Case)

Land rights then and now
47 *Gila River Indian Community v. the U.S. Court of Claims* (1974) 204
48 *U.S. v. Pueblo of San Ildefonso* (1975) 205 at p. 651
49 *Guerin v. the Queen* (1985) 13 Dominion Law Reports 336
50 *United States v. Seminole Indians* (1967) 180 U.S. Court of Claims 375
51 *Western Sahara Case (1975) International Court of Justice* Reports 39

Definition of and dealings in land
52 *Wilkinson v. Proud* (1843) 11 M & W 33, 152 ER 704
53 *Williamson v. Wootton* (1855) 3 Drew 210, 61 ER 883
54 *Cox v. Glue* (1848) 5CB 533, 136 ER 987
55 Re Haven Gold Mining Co., (1882) 20 Ch.D. 151, (1881) All ER 585
56 *Chirnside v. Registrar of Titles* (1921) VLR 406

Property
57 *City of Red Dear v. Western General Electric Co.* (1917) 34 DLR 406, (1917) 2WWR 450
58 *Harris v. Tong* (1930) 65 Ontario Law Reports 133, (1930) 3 DLR 32
59 Re Lunnes (1919) 46 OLR; 51 DLR 114

Deprivation of property
60 *Ranlogan v. The Mayor, Alderman and Burgesses of San Fernando* (1986) LRC (Const.) 377
61 *Hael Freres Ltd v. Minister for Housing etc.* (1988) LRC (Const.) 472
62 *Norton v. Public Service Commission* (1988) LRC (Const.) 944
63 *Sociéte United Docks & Ors. v. Govt. of Mauritius* and *Marine Workers Union & Ors. v. Mauritius Marine Authority & Ors.* (1885) LRC (Const.) 801

Public interest
64 Re Loisille and Town of Red Dear (1907) 7 WLR 42 (Alta)

Public Officer
65 *R. v. Whitaker* (1914) 3KB 1283

Public Office
66 Re Mirams (1891) 1 QB 594

Public purpose
67 *K.K. Kochunni v. States of Madras and Kerala* (1960) All India Reports 1080
68 *State of Madhya Pradesh v. Ranojirao Shinde* (1968) AIR 1053
69 Bank Nationalisation Case *(R.C. Cooper v. Union)* (1970) AIR 564.
70 *Mersey Docks and Harbor Board Trustees v. Cameron* (1865) 11 HL Cas
71 *Greig v. University of Edinburgh* (1868) KR 1 Sc & D 348
72 *Bank Voor Handel en Scheepvaart NV v. Slatford* (1953) 1 QB 248
73 *St MacNissi's College (trustees) v. Valuation Commissioner* (1957) W.I. 25

74 *Chandler v. DPP* (1962) 3 All ER 142

Mining rights as interests in land
75 *Tainui Maori Trust Board v. A.G.* (1989) 2 NZLR 513
76 Re Associated Portland Cement Manufactuers Ltd's Application (1965) 2 All ER 547

Constitutional reasonableness
77 *Hunter v. Southern* (1984) 2 SCR 145; 11 DLR (4th) 641
78 *Edwards v. Attorney General for Canada* (1930) AC 124
79 *Minister of Home Affairs v. Fisher* (1980) AC 319
80 *McCullock v. Maryland* (1819) 17 U.S. (5 Wheat) 316

Vested rights
81 *Smith v. Hill* 73 ALR 2d 540
82 *People Ex re Foot v. Clark* 253
83 *Eitel v. Lindlheimer* 124 ALR 1472
84 *Hegerty v. Administrator,* Unemployment Compensation Act, 20 ALR 2d 960
85 *State Ex Rel Ricco v. Biggs* 38 ALR 2d 720
86 *Averne Bay Construction Co. v. Thatcher* 117 ALR 1110
87 *Maine v. R.B. Johnson* 46 ALR 3d 1414
88 *State v. Union Oil Company* 151 ME 438

Eminent domain
89 *Bountiful City v. Frank Deluca* 72 ALR 657
90 *George Murrison v. Irma Fenstermacher* 7 ALR 2d 1360
91 *Groesbeck v. Seeley* 13 Mich 329
92 *Superior Oil Company v. Alfred Foote* 37 ALR 2d 415
93 *Albert H. Jacobson et al. v. Superior Court of the County of Sonoma* Dept. 2. 29 ALR 1399

Arbitrary search and seizure
94 *Jones v. United States* 78 ALR 2d 233

United Nations Mandate and Trust Territories – advisory opinions
95 International status of South West Afric (1950) ICJ 128
96 Legal consequences for States of the Continued Presence of South Africa in

Namibia (South West Africa) notwithstanding Security Council Resolution 276 (1970), 1971 ICJ 16

Books and other materials

1. R.T Latham quoted by V. Windeyer, "A Birthright and Inheritance", *Tasmanian University Law Review*, 1 Nov. 1962, p. 635
2. J. Bouvier, *A Law Dictionary*, 11th Ed., Philadelphia, 1866, p. 258
3. Hugo Grotius, *The Rights of War and Peace*, 2 Vols., London, 1738, 2, p. 550
4. Hugo Grotius, *The Freedom of the Seas,* Oxford University Press, New York, 1916, p. 11
5. J.G. Heineccius, *A Methodical System of International Law,* 2 Vols., London, 1743, 1, p. 182
6. R. Phillimore, *Commentaries upon International Law,* 4 Vols., London, 1854, 7, p. 289
7. W.E. Hall, *A Treatise on Public International Law*, 8th ed., Clarendon Press, Oxford, 1924, p. 125
8. H. Taylor, *A Treatise on International Public Law,* Callaghan, Chicago, 1901, p. 128
9. K. Roberts-Wray, *Commonwealth and Colonial Law,* Stephens & Co., London, 1966, p. 631
10. G. Bennett, "Aboriginal Title in Common Law", *Buffalo Law Review,* 27, 1978, pp. 617-35
11. T.J. Lawrence, *The Principles of International Law,* Macmillan, London, 1910, pp. 156-7
12. E. de Vattel, *The Law of Nations,* 3 Vols., Washington, 1916, 3, p. 84
13. C. Wolff, *Jus Gentium* (The Law of Nations), Clarendon Press, Oxford, 1934, pp. 157-60
14. W. Blackstone, *Commentaries on the Laws of England,* 3 Vols., 18th ed., London, 1823, 2
15. J. Legge (ed.), *A Selection of Supreme Court Cases,* 2 Vols., Sydney, 1896, 1
16. Von Savigny, *Treatise on Possession,* 6th ed., London, 1848, p. 10
17. United Nations Charter
18. Universal Declaration of Human Rights
19. United States Constitution
20. Constitution of India
21. European Convention on Human Rights

22 Prosser in *Law of Torts,* 2nd Edition 1955, ... on privacy
23 *Privacy and Human Rights,* edited by A. H. Robertson
24 *This is our Land – The Mohawk Revolt at Oka,* by Craig Maclaine & Michael Baxendale, 1990, published by Optimum Publishing International Inc., Montreal, Canada
25 *Last Stand of the Lubicon Cree,* by John Goddard 1991, published by Douglas & McIntyre Ltd., Vancouver, Canada
26 *Law and Policy in Petroleum Development: Changing Relations between Transnationals and Governments,* by Kamal Hossain, Nichols Publishing Company (USA), 1979

PNG & Australian materials

27 Law Reform Commission's Working Paper on Resources
28 *Australian Mining & Petroleum Laws,* 2nd ed., by J.R.S. Forbes and A.G. Lang
29 *Annotated Constitution of PNG,* by Brian Brunton and Duncan Colquhoun-Kerr
30 Final Report of the Constitutional Planning Committee
31 A paper entitled "Proposed Changes to Mining Legislation in Papua New Guinea" by Diana Lee Dalton, the Minerals Policy Officer of the Department of Minerals and Energy, presented at the PNG Resources Conference held in Port Moresby in June 1988 ("the Resources Conference")
32 A paper entitled "Property Rights, Landowner Participation and Conflict in the PNG Mining Industry", by Christopher Warrilow, the Petroleum Registrar with DME at the said Resources Conference
33 A paper entitled "Local Attitudes to Mineral Exploration and Mining in North Solomons Province", by J. Tsinoung, D. Itta and R. Rogerson, also presented at the said Resources Conference
34 The closing address of the then Secretary for Minerals and Energy, Mr William Searson, at the said Resources Conference
35 Institute of National Affairs (PNG) publication of 10th June 1981 entitled "Land Policy and Economic Development in Papua New Guinea"
36 Australian National University publication of "An Independent Review of the Economy of Papua New Guinea" by Goodman, Lepani and Morawetz, dated 1985
37 Article entitled "Land Mobilisation programme in Papua New Guinea" by Professor R.W. James, (1990) 18 *MLJ,* 38
38 PNG Law Reform Commission publication entitled "Land Law and Policy in Papua New Guinea" by Professor R.W. James, *Monograph,* No. 5 of 1985

39 Law Reform Commision's occasional paper No. 20 (1990) entitled "New Directions in Resources Management for Papua New Guinea"
40 Bank of Papua New Guinea publication entitled "Guide to Exchange Control in Papua New Guinea"
41 League of Nations Mandate
42 UN Trusteeship Agreement with Australia in respect to New Guinea
43 *Security and Survival,* by Dr. Cammileri and Dr. Teichmann
44 Various Law Dictionaries
45 Paper entitled "Land Policy and Economic Development in Papua New Guinea", by Trebilcock and Knetsh (1981), *MLJ,* Vol. 9
46 *Introduction to the Law of Land Use in Papua New Guinea* by A.D. Miller, Assistant Surveyor General, Department of Lands and Physical Planning, September 1990
47 "Land Disputes in PNG: A Colonial Legacy and Post Independence Solutions" by Dr John Mugambwa, 1987, *MLJ,* Vol. 15, 94
48 *The Law of the Land* by Henry Reynolds, 1987, published by Penguin Books Australia Ltd
49 *A Time to Plant and a Time to Uproot: A history of agriculture in Papua New Guinea,* edited by Donald Denoon and Catherine Snowden for the Department of Primary Industry, Institute of Papua New Guinea Studies publication

Papua New Guinea legislations
1 The National Constitution
2 Papua New Guinea Act (No. 9 of 1949 – Commonwealth of Australia)
3 Mining Act Ch. No. 195
4 Petroleum Act Ch. No. 198
5 Land Act Ch. No. 184
6 Land Registration Act 1981
7 Wuvulu Land Acquisition Act
8 Water Resources Act
9 Forestry Act
10 Forestry Private Dealings Act
11 Central Banking Act
12 Statute of Frauds and Limitations Act

Abbreviations

Commonwealth and UN Legal Abbreviations

AC	[UK] Appeal Cases
AIR	[India] All India Reports
ALJR	[Australian] Australian Law Journal Reports
All ER	[UK] All England Reports
Ch.D.	[UK] Chancery Division Cases
CLR	[Australian] Commonwealth Law Reports
DLR	[Canadian] Dominion Law Reports
ER	[UK] English Reports
FLR	[Australian] Federal Law Reports
ICJ	[UN] International Court of Justice
KBD	[UK] Kings Bench Division Cases
LRC	[Commonwealth] Law Reports of the Commonwealth
NZLR	[NZ] New Zealand Law Reports
PNGLR	[PNG] Papua New Guinea Law Reports
QBD	[UK] Queens Bench Division Cases
VLR	[Australia] Victorian Law Reports